Kidspiration® in the Classroom:
Math Made Visual

NUMBER AND
OPERATIONS

ALGEBRA

MEASUREMENT

GEOMETRY

Includes 30
Lesson Plans!

GRADES K-5

Inspiration®
SOFTWARE, INC

Publisher: Mona L. Westhaver

Author: Meg Courtnage

Contributors: Mary Beth Saddoris and Andrea Sutherland

Editors: Erin Antonius, Amy Chan, Mary Beth Saddoris and Andrea Sutherland

Layout/Design: Kevin Jaquette

Introduction to *Kidspiration® in the Classroom: Math Made Visual*

Inspiration Software®, Inc. strives to support improvements in education and make a positive difference in students' lives. This book is part of our family of K-12 visual learning software tools and curriculum materials that help students learn to think and master key concepts. We value teachers, their time, and their commitment, and we strive to partner in their success.

Kidspiration® in the Classroom: Math Made Visual supports teachers as they help students develop mathematical concepts, skills, thinking and reasoning. Covering the K-5 grade range, *Kidspiration in the Classroom: Math Made Visual* offers 30 lesson plans aligned to NCTM standards and designed specifically to support K-5 math instruction using Kidspiration 3.

Lessons focus on core content strands, including number and operations, algebra, measurement, and geometry, in contexts that promote problem solving, reasoning and communication. Utilizing activities created in Kidspiration's Picture View and Math View, these lessons help students develop conceptual understanding while communicating their thinking with pictures, models, words, numbers and math symbols.

Each easy-to-use lesson includes suggested grade levels, standards alignment, a lesson description, step-by-step instructions, ideas for assessment, and adaptations for differentiating instruction and extending the lesson.

Standards are reprinted with permission from *Principles and Standards for School Mathematics*, 2000, by the National Council of Teachers of Mathematics (NCTM). All rights reserved.

Kidspiration® in the Classroom: Math Made Visual
Lesson Grid and Table of Contents

Lesson Name	Page	Grade Level						Content Standards			
		K	1	2	3	4	5	Number & Operations	Algebra	Geometry	Measurement
Multi-Digit Addition	76			√	√			√			
Subtraction with Regrouping	82			√	√			√			
Comparing Areas	88			√	√	√	√			√	√
Division Stories	92				√	√		√	√		
Parts and Wholes	98				√	√		√			
Building and Estimating Fractions	104				√	√	√	√			
Comparing Fractions	108				√	√	√	√	√		
Equivalent Fractions	112				√	√	√	√			
Finding Factors with Rectangles	116				√	√	√	√		√	√
Flips, Slides and Turns	122				√	√	√			√	
Adding Fractions with Unlike Denominators	128					√	√	√			
Area Models for Multiplication	134					√	√	√	√	√	√
Long Division	140					√	√	√			
Mixed Numbers and Improper Fractions	146					√	√	√			
Representing and Comparing Decimals	152					√	√	√			

Counting Fish

✦ **Grade Levels: K-1 (Ages 5-7)**

✦ **NCTM Principles and Standards for School Mathematics**

- Counts with understanding and recognizes "how many" in sets of objects
- Connects number words and numerals to the quantities they represent, using various physical models and representations
- Understands various meanings of addition of whole numbers
- Illustrates general principles and properties of operations, such as commutativity, using specific numbers
- Models situations that involve the addition of whole numbers, using objects and pictures

Note: These standards are listed with the permission of the National Council of Teachers of Mathematics (NCTM). NCTM does not endorse the content or validity of these alignments.

Description

Counting is fundamental to students' success with number and operations in the early grades. Concrete models can help students represent numbers, develop number sense and bring meaning to written symbols. In this **Kidspiration®** lesson, students will work in **Picture View** to practice basic counting techniques as they produce sets of given sizes, connecting number words and numerals to the quantities they represent through the movement of symbols. They will informally solve basic addition problems by counting the number in combined sets and developing strategies such as "counting on." The activity supports students' understanding of the connection between counting and addition.

Instructions

1. The resources for this lesson can be found at the following location: **Kidspiration 3 Teacher menu>Teacher Resources Online>Lesson Plans>Grades K-2 Math>Counting Fish**. Save the Zip file and open the included *Counting Fish.kia* activity.

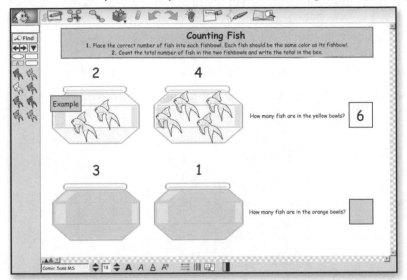

Explain to students that they are going to fill the fishbowls with fish. Point to the example and show that the number above each fishbowl tells how many fish should go in that bowl. Each fish should be the same color as its fishbowl; for example, in the yellow fishbowls there are yellow fish. When they have filled both of the fishbowls of a single color, they will find the total number of fish in the two bowls.

2. The activity contains eight fishbowl problems, accessible by scrolling. It may be helpful to complete one problem together as a class before students work independently. Point to the first orange fishbowl and ask students how many fish should go inside the bowl, allowing students to connect the numeral to its number word. What color of fish should go in the bowl? Demonstrate how to drag three orange fish from the **Symbol palette**, having students count aloud "1, 2, 3" as you place each fish in the fishbowl. Point to each fish in the bowl and count them in an order that is different from the order in which they were brought out, confirming with students that counting objects in a different order does not alter the quantity. Repeat this process for the second orange fishbowl. Explain to students that they must now write the total number of orange fish, from both bowls, in the orange box. Allow students to describe how they find the total number.

3. Have students work independently to complete *Counting Fish.kia*. Ask that students count aloud as they work on the activity. Saying the number words aloud as they move objects helps students establish a one-to-one correspondence between the number word and the quantity that it represents. Circulate while students are working, taking note of how they find their totals. When finding the total number of fish in the blue fishbowl, for example, some students may count "1, 2, 3, 4, 5" for one fishbowl and then "6, 7" for the second fishbowl. Others may not have to re-count the fish in the first fishbowl and may simply point to the first fishbowl and say "5" and then point to the second fishbowl and count on "6, 7." These students demonstrate an early understanding of the "counting on" strategy for addition.

4. (Optional) Students who finish early can switch to **Writing View** and write number words next to each fish.

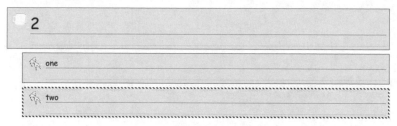

5. Close the lesson by going over each problem or having students present their work. Include the following questions in your discussion:

    *   How did you find your totals? (Show the strategy of "counting on" and determine that this yields the same answer as counting each fish individually.)

    *   How did you represent the number 0 in the purple fishbowl? What was the total number of fish in the purple fishbowls if one of the bowls had 0 fish?

- What did you notice about the red and green fishbowls? Why did they both have a total of 9 fish? Does it matter whether the 6 fish are counted first or the 3 fish are counted first?

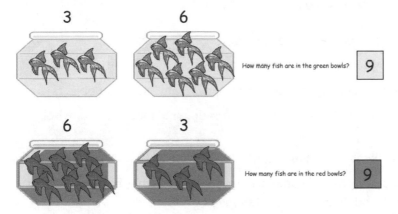

- For each pair of fishbowls, which fishbowl had more fish? Have students use language such as "less than," "more than" and "equal to" to compare the quantities.

 Assessment

- Check activities for correct quantities and numerals. See *Counting Fish Exemplar.kid* from the previously downloaded Zip file for a sample completed activity.

- Assess students on their ability to show a one-to-one correspondence between number words and quantities as they count aloud.

 Adaptations

- Students who are ready for the symbolic notation of addition can use a **Math Text Box** to write number sentences or expressions that match each fishbowl representation.

- The labels on the fishbowls can be changed from numerals to number words, such as "four," to give students practice relating number words to quantities.

Ordering Sets

★ **Grade Levels: K-1 (Ages 5-7)**

★ **NCTM Principles and Standards for School Mathematics**

- Orders objects by number

- Counts with understanding and recognizes "how many" in sets of objects

- Develops an understanding of the relative position and magnitude of whole numbers

- Recognizes and names two-dimensional shapes

- Connects number words and numerals to the quantities they represent, using various physical models and representations

Note: These standards are listed with the permission of the National Council of Teachers of Mathematics (NCTM). NCTM does not endorse the content or validity of these alignments.

Description

In this lesson, students will use **Kidspiration Pattern Blocks™** in an activity that integrates counting, comparing, ordering and shape recognition. In the context of solving the mystery of the missing shapes, students will choose quantities of shapes based on clues about "more than" and "less than." They will discuss the possibility of more than one solution, review the names of shapes, count aloud as they fill boxes with shapes and label groups with corresponding numerals. After solving their mysteries, students will compare their solutions.

Instructions

1. Begin the lesson by making a comparison between yourself and a friend. For example, "Today I am wearing four pockets. 1, 2, 3, 4. My friend John is wearing more pockets than me. How many pockets could John have?" After eliciting suggestions from students, add a comparative statement about another friend. For example, "My other friend Emily is wearing pockets. The number of pockets that Emily has is less than the number of pockets that I have. How many pockets could Emily have?" After discussing that there are multiple solutions, but that only some may be reasonable, explain to students that today they will be working to solve the mystery of the missing shapes.

2. The resources for this lesson can be found at the following location: **Kidspiration 3 Teacher menu>Teacher Resources Online>Lesson Plans>Grades K-2 Math>Ordering Sets**. Save the Zip file and open the included *Ordering Sets.kia* activity.

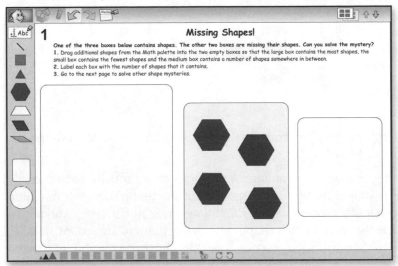

Complete the first page of this activity together as a class. Ask students which box has shapes in it, and the name and number of the shapes that it contains (4 hexagons). Show how to click inside the **Math SuperGrouper™** to label the box with the number 4. Now point out that there are two empty boxes, a small box and a large box, and that their shapes are missing. We know that the large box contained more hexagons than the medium box, and the small box contained fewer hexagons than the medium box. Tell students that their job is to solve the mystery of the missing shapes and fill the empty boxes with hexagons.

3. Ask students to think first about how many hexagons they would put in the small box. Elicit suggestions from several students. Some students might want to put 3 hexagons in the box, while others might want 2, 1, or 0 hexagons. Pose the following question to students: If the small box had fewer hexagons in it than the medium box, can there be more than one correct answer? Why? Have students name quantities that could *not* go in the small box, and have them describe why, using phrases like *less than, more than* or *equal to*. Choose one correct quantity suggested by a student, and show how to drag hexagons from the **Math palette** into the smallest box. Model counting aloud as you move the shapes into the box, as this allows students to establish a one-to-one correspondence, through movement, with the counted number and the quantity that it represents. Label the small box with the counted number, and repeat the process of decision-making for the large box.

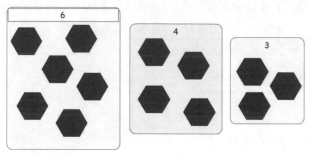

Did we solve the mystery, or did we just find one possibility? Is it possible to solve the mystery based on what we know?

4. Have students work independently to complete all six pages of the activity. Each page will use a different shape, and both the initial placement of shapes (in the small, medium or large box) and the order of the boxes will vary. Circulate while students are working, encouraging them to say the names of the shapes aloud. Ask them to also count aloud as they move shapes into the boxes, and to describe how they chose the number of shapes that they did.

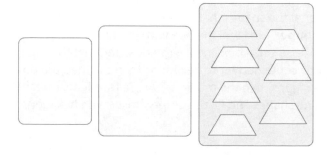

Note: If you do not wish to introduce students to the names *rhombus* and *trapezoid*, students can describe the shape by its number of sides, and explain how they know why these four-sided shapes are neither squares nor rectangles.

5. Have several students present their completed activities. For each problem, ask if other students solved the mystery in a different way. How many possibilities are there? What number of shapes do we know could *not* have been in the box?

Assessment

- Check completed activities for correct ordering of quantities and corresponding numerals. See *Ordering Sets Exemplar.kid* from the previously downloaded Zip file for a sample completed activity.

- Assess students on their oral participation, including their ability to name and describe shapes, count aloud, use comparative language, and reason about multiple solutions.

Adaptations

- Have students label boxes with the names of shapes as well as the quantity.

- Students who are ready to learn about relational symbols can compare the boxes using the **Greater Than** or **Less Than** buttons from the **Bottom** toolbar, placing symbols between the boxes.

- Have students write number words instead of numerals in each of the boxes.

- Rather than keeping the activity open-ended, modify the activity instructions to include more specific clues. For example, require that the quantity in each box be consecutive (3, 4 and 5) or skip a number (2, 4, 6).

Sorting Shapes

✦ **Grade Levels: K-1 (Ages 5-7)**

✦ **NCTM Principles and Standards for School Mathematics**

- Recognizes, names, compares and sorts two-dimensional shapes
- Describes attributes and parts of two-dimensional shapes
- Counts with understanding and recognizes "how many" in sets of objects
- Recognizes geometric shapes and structures in the environment

Note: These standards are listed with the permission of the National Council of Teachers of Mathematics (NCTM). NCTM does not endorse the content or validity of these alignments.

Description

In elementary school, young students refine and extend their understanding of concepts of shapes. Though concrete explorations and discussions, students find language to describe and compare shapes and their attributes. In this series of six **Kidspiration® Picture View** activities, students will sort two-dimensional shapes into suitcases. Shapes will be sorted by color, number of corners, name, roundness, number of sides and whether or not the shapes can be found in their classroom. The activities can be completed in any order and can even be spread throughout a school year.

Instructions

1. Introduce the lesson by telling students about a girl named Sydney who plans to visit Shapeland. For each trip to Shapeland, she is instructed to pack her suitcases in different ways. Today students will help Sydney with her packing.

2. The resources for this lesson can be found at the following location: **Kidspiration 3 Teacher menu>Teacher Resources Online>Lesson Plans>Grades K-2 Math>Sorting Shapes**. Save the Zip file and open any of the six included student activities: *Sorting by Color.kia, Sorting by Corners.kia, Sorting by I see it.kia, Sorting by Name.kia, Sorting by Roundness.kia* or *Sorting by Sides.kia*.

   In each activity, students will decide how to sort shapes into labeled suitcases. Shapes will be dragged from the **Symbol palette** into the suitcases.

   Note: Depending on time, computer availability and the skill level of your students, you may choose to do one of the activities as a class and then have students work individually or in pairs to complete the remaining activities. Alternatively, all activities can be done either as a whole group or by students individually.

3. For each activity, include the following sets of questions in your discussion. If completing the activity as a class, questions can be asked after each activity has been finished. If students are working individually to complete the activities, ask questions while circulating and also in the class follow-up discussion.

Sorting by Color.kia activity

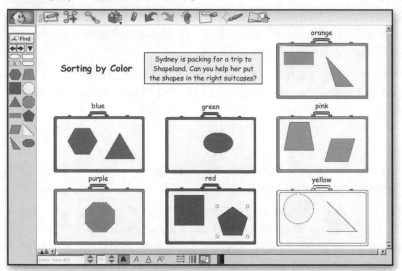

- How many shapes are in each suitcase?

- Which suitcase(s) has the most shapes in it?

- Which suitcase(s) has the least shapes in it?

- Were any suitcases empty?

- Can you name a color that you do *not* see?

Sorting by Corners.kia activity

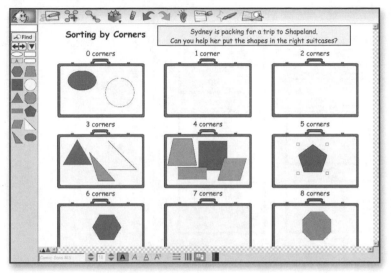

Note: The word "angle" can be used instead of "corner."

- How can you tell if a shape has a "corner?"

- How many shapes are in each suitcase?

- Which suitcase(s) has the most shapes in it?

- Which suitcase(s) has the least shapes in it?

- Were any suitcases empty?

- Do you think that shapes can have 1 corner? How about 2 corners?

- If we changed the word "corner" on each suitcase to "side," would we have to put the shapes in different suitcases? What do you notice, for example, about shapes that have 3 corners? How many sides do they have?

Sorting by Name.kia activity

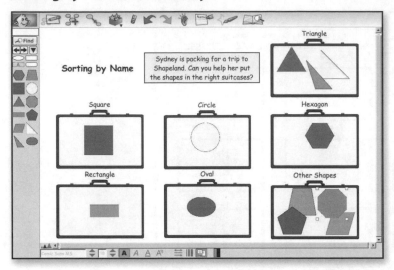

Note: The labels on the suitcases can be changed to reflect names of shapes that students are expected to know and/or learn at the current grade level.

- How do you know that a shape is a triangle? A square? A circle? (Continue asking about how they know the other shapes.)

- How many shapes are in each suitcase?

- Which suitcase(s) has the most shapes in it?

- Which suitcase(s) has the least shapes in it?

- Do all of the triangles look the same? How are they the same? How are they different?

- How is a rectangle different from a square?

- What do the pink shapes have in common with the square and the rectangle? How are they different?

- How is an oval different from a circle?

Sorting by Roundness.kia activity

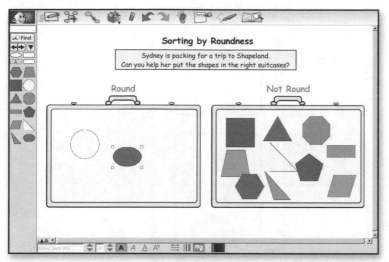

- What does it mean if a shape is round?
- How do you decide that a shape is *not* round?
- How many shapes are in each suitcase?
- Which suitcase has the most shapes in it?
- Which suitcase has the least shapes in it?
- Is either of suitcases empty?
- The oval and the circle are both round, but how are they different?
- What do you see around the classroom that you could put in the "Round" suitcase to fill it up?
- Do you think you see more round shapes in the world or more shapes with straight edges?

Sorting by Sides.kia activity

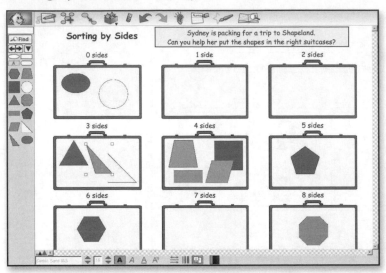

Note: Among mathematicians, a circle is sometimes considered to have 0 sides, 1 side, or an infinite number of sides. It is very important that before shapes are sorted, you define what a side is for the purposes of the activity. If you define a side to refer to a straight edge, for example, then a circle has 0 sides.

- What does the word "side" mean?
- How many shapes are in each suitcase?
- Were any suitcases empty?
- Which suitcase(s) has the most shapes in it?
- Which suitcase(s) has the least shapes in it?
- Do you think shapes can have 2 sides?
- Do you think shapes can have 7 sides? Can you draw one?
- Do all of the shapes in the "3 sides" suitcase have the same name? What is it?
- Do all of the shapes in the "4 sides" suitcase have the same name?

Sorting by I see it.kia activity

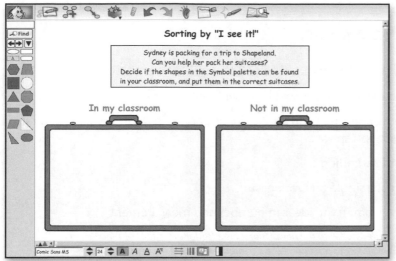

Questions and discussion will depend on what shapes are found in the classroom.

Assessment

- Assess completed activities for correct sorting of shapes.
- Assess students on their ability to verbally describe and reason about shapes and attributes.

Adaptations

- On each activity, change the name "Sydney" to a different name of a student in the class.
- Differentiate instruction by assigning students different activities.
- Add sorting activities that include 3-dimensional shapes. Use the *Shapes* Symbol library under *Math & Numbers* or create your own custom library.

Exploring Symmetry

★ **Grade Levels: K-2 (Ages 5-8)**

★ **NCTM Principles and Standards for School Mathematics**

- Recognizes and creates shapes that have symmetry
- Describes, names, interprets and applies ideas about direction, distance and relative position in navigating space
- Counts with understanding
- Uses repetition of a single unit to measure
- Relates ideas in geometry to ideas in number and measurement

Note: These standards are listed with the permission of the National Council of Teachers of Mathematics (NCTM). NCTM does not endorse the content or validity of these alignments.

Description

In elementary school, students often get practice identifying or drawing lines of symmetry. They have fewer opportunities, however, to be actively engaged in constructing designs with line symmetry, a process that strengthens their geometric and spatial reasoning skills. In this lesson, students will use **Kidspiration Color Tiles™** to explore line symmetry by completing designs and building their own designs. They will discuss methods for determining reflective symmetry, such as counting distance or folding, and develop an understanding of symmetrical figures.

Instructions

1. Open the lesson by asking students what happens when they look in the mirror. If they raise their hand, what happens to their image in the mirror? If they turn their head, what happens to their image in the mirror? Discuss what it means for something to be symmetrical, and define a line of symmetry. Ask students if they can find anything in the classroom that is symmetrical, and to describe where its line of symmetry would fall.

2. The resources for this lesson can be found at the following location: **Kidspiration 3 Teacher menu>Teacher Resources Online>Lesson Plans>Grades K-2 Math>Exploring Symmetry**. Save the Zip file and open the included *Exploring Symmetry.kia* activity.

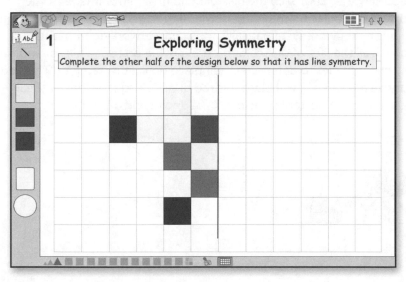

3. It might be helpful to start the first page of the activity together as a class. Explain to students that they are going to complete the design so that it has line symmetry. Students might benefit from thinking about it as building a mirror image. Ask student volunteers to come up, one at a time, and add one color tile to the workspace that will help build the mirror image. As they place the tile, ask students to describe how they decided on the tile's location. Place one tile in an incorrect location as a counterexample. Ask students to explain why the tile is placed incorrectly, and what would happen if we were to fold on the line.

4. Depending on computer availability, have students work individually or in pairs to complete all eight pages of the activity, *Exploring Symmetry.kia*. Circulate as students are working, and notice how they approach the task of building a mirror image. Some students may use trial and error, placing tiles randomly and then deciding if the placement is correct. Other students might work systematically; for example, working from the top row down or starting with all the tiles of one color before moving on to the tiles of another color. Some students will count tiles to determine their placement. For example, "That red tile is 1, 2, 3 squares above the line, so I will place this red tile 1, 2, 3 squares below the line." These students are learning the important principles of midpoint and distance that underlie symmetry.

5. On pages 7 and 8 of the activity, students will start with only a line of symmetry and build their own design with line symmetry. Students who are working in pairs might take turns, having one student place a tile and the other student place its mirror image on the other side of the line.

6. Ask each student to select a favorite from the designs that they built, and print it out to share with the class. Use folding to demonstrate that each design has line symmetry. As students are showcasing their designs, include the following prompts in the class discussion:

- Was it easier to work with horizontal or vertical lines? (Because students see many objects in their environment with vertical line symmetry, such as people, plants, houses and animals, they may have more difficulty with horizontal line symmetry.)

- How did you determine where to place a tile? What other ways did you know that both halves matched besides folding?

- Did any designs have a second line of symmetry?

Assessment

- Students can be assessed on their completed activities, checking for correct number and placement of tiles. See *Exploring Symmetry Exemplar.kid* from the previously downloaded Zip file for a sample completed activity

- Assess students on their contributions to class and pair discussions. How well can they articulate symmetry and explain how to place tiles when building a mirror image?

Adaptations

- For pages 7 and 8 of the activity, where students are building their own designs with line symmetry, you may want to require a minimum or maximum number of tiles to use.

- By unlocking the line of symmetry on pages 7 and 8 and using the **Resize Manipulatives** button on the **Bottom** toolbar, students can work with smaller color tiles to build larger designs with more complexity.

- For advanced work with symmetry, students can use pattern blocks to build designs with symmetry. Go to **Kidspiration Starter>Activities>Math** and open the *Symmetry.kia* activity.

Measuring with Tiles

✦ **Grade Levels: K-2 (Ages 5-8)**

✦ **NCTM Principles and Standards for School Mathematics**

- Recognizes the attribute of length and compares and orders objects accordingly
- Understands how to measure using non-standard units
- Connects numerals to the quantities they represent, using various physical models and representations
- Uses repetition of a single unit to measure something larger than the unit

Note: These standards are listed with the permission of the National Council of Teachers of Mathematics (NCTM). NCTM does not endorse the content or validity of these alignments.

Description

In this activity, students will work with **Kidspiration Color Tiles™** to measure lengths using non-standard units. Students will have the opportunity to make estimates, count, measure and compare. As an informal introduction to concepts of rounding, students will also work with lengths that are in between whole number units, and discuss how to determine lengths to the nearest tile.

Instructions

1. Prior to beginning the lesson, read aloud a book that emphasizes distance or length, such as *The Bravest Dog Ever: The True Story of Balto* by Natalie Standiford.

   Note: Reading this particular book is not required to complete the lesson. Begin by discussing any story or examples from students' lives involving distance or length. Discuss both short and long distances, and how students determine whether a distance is short or long.

2. The resources for this lesson can be found at the following location: **Kidspiration 3 Teacher menu>Teacher Resources Online>Lesson Plans>Grades K-2 Math>Measuring with Tiles**. Save the Zip file and open the included *Measuring with Tiles.kia* activity. Read the directions aloud, explaining to students that they are going to help Balto the Dog and his sled team measure and compare the lengths of eight different trips.

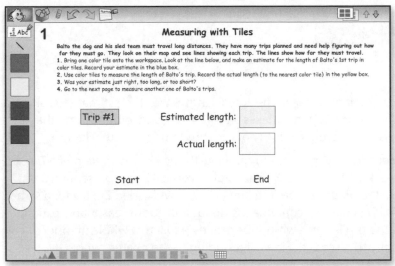

3. Find the length of the first trip together. Point to the line that indicates the map distance, and bring out a color tile from the **Math palette**. Ask students to think about how many color tiles, snapped together, it would take to make a train as long as the length of the line. Emphasize that an estimate is different from a wild guess. Call on several students for their estimate, asking how they made their estimate. Choose one estimate to record in the blue text box.

4. Ask for a student volunteer to use color tiles to measure the length to the nearest whole tile, counting aloud as they bring tiles onto the workspace. The volunteer may want to try lengths of both five and six color tiles. If so, the student can place one row of color tiles above the line and one row of a different length below the line to help them make their decision. Some students may claim that the length in color tiles is neither 5 nor 6, while others may claim that it is "a little less than" 6, or "a little more than" 5. Encourage this discussion, as it opens up communication about quantities between whole numbers, setting the foundation for later work with fractions and decimals. Push students to pick the *best* answer in whole tiles, and then ask several students to defend their choice.

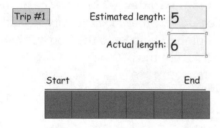

5. Ask students to compare their estimate to the actual length. Was the estimate too short, just right, or too long? Ask students what makes an estimate good, emphasizing that an estimate can still be very good even if it does not turn out to be the actual length.

6. Have students work independently or in pairs to complete the activity. *Measuring with Tiles.kia* contains eight pages, each with a different horizontal or vertical line representing a trip distance. See *Measuring Exemplar.kid* from the previously downloaded Zip file for a sample completed activity. While circulating, continue the discussion about reasonable estimates. Also, since many of Balto's trip lengths will not be exactly equal to a whole number of color tiles, take the opportunity to discuss the idea of rounding to the nearest whole tile.

7. Once students have finished, have a class discussion that includes the following prompts:

    - How did you estimate the lengths?

    - How did your estimates compare to actual lengths? Did your estimates get better further into the activity?

    - Were there any trips that you had difficulty measuring? (Trip #6 is 3½ tiles in length. It may be worth discussing whether 3 or 4 is a better answer.)

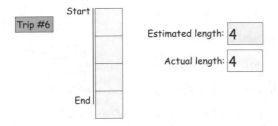

Assessment

- Individual students or pairs can each present their work on one of Balto's eight trips. Assess students on their reasoning, communication and results.

- Assess students on their participation in class discussions and on their completed activities, checking for good estimates and accurate measurements.

Adaptations

- Students who are familiar with basic fractions (halves, thirds and fourths) may use fractions to describe lengths. The concept of rounding to the nearest half can be introduced.

Pattern Trains

★ **Grade Levels: K-2 (Ages 5-8)**

★ **NCTM Principles and Standards for School Mathematics**

- Recognizes, describes and extends patterns such as sequences of shapes
- Analyzes how repeating patterns are generated
- Recognizes and names two-dimensional shapes
- Investigates the results of putting together two-dimensional shapes
- Counts with understanding and recognizes "how many" in sets of objects

Note: *These standards are listed with the permission of the National Council of Teachers of Mathematics (NCTM). NCTM does not endorse the content or validity of these alignments.*

Description

Young students develop algebraic concepts early through work with patterns, building the foundation for using symbolic rules to represent patterns in later years. In this lesson, students will use **Kidspiration Pattern Blocks™** to build and extend repeating patterns. The lesson plan offers opportunities for students to develop the following concepts: patterning with repetition, composing shapes, counting, shape identification, estimation and prediction. Options and adaptations throughout the lesson make it appropriate and modifiable for the K-2 grade span.

Instructions

1. Introduce the lesson by asking students to think of things they see or hear that repeat. For example, can they think of any songs in which words are repeated? Are there patterns that they see on the floor or the wall, at home or at school? Can they find patterns on their clothing, with shapes or colors? Explain to students that today they are going to build trains with patterns.

2. The resources for this activity can be found at the following location: **Kidspiration 3 Teacher menu>Teacher Resources Online>Lesson Plans>Grades K-2 Math>Pattern Trains**. Save the Zip file and open the included *Pattern Trains.kia* activity.

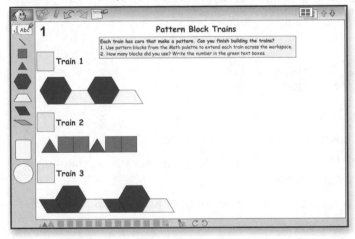

3. Complete the first problem together as a class. Explain to students that the blocks represent the cars of a train, and that the cars form a pattern. Ask students to "think, pair, share" about Train 1. What do they notice? Give them time to think quietly before vocalizing their ideas in pairs. Then ask the pairs to share what they noticed with the class. Students may share any of the following: "It has 4 cars," "I see 2 different shapes," "I see blue-yellow-blue-yellow," "It repeats, blue-yellow, blue-yellow." If students are familiar with the names of shapes, they might offer "I see hexagon-trapezoid-hexagon-trapezoid."

   (Optional) Ask students to find the smallest unit that gets repeated in the train pattern. It may help students to recite the colors or shapes aloud, for example, "blue-yellow-blue-yellow" to determine the pattern's repeating group, or *core*. They can also mark the core with the **Cross-Out Stamp** located on the **Bottom** toolbar.

4. Explain to students that they are going to follow the same pattern to finish building the train across the workspace. As a "think, pair, share," ask students to estimate the total number of blocks in the completed train. Some students may pick a number, such as 6, simply because it is their favorite number, or their age. As needed, encourage students to pick a number based on how many blocks they think will fit across the workspace. Have students explain and share their reasoning.

5. Ask for a student volunteer to extend the train using pattern blocks. Have them reason aloud as they place the blocks. For example, "A blue always comes after a yellow. That was a yellow shape, so next I use a blue shape." When they are finished, have them point to each shape and count aloud to find the total number of blocks used to form the train. Select the green text box and type the total number.

12 Train 1

6. Discuss the following with students:

   • How did your estimate compare to the actual total number of blocks?

   • Are there other ways to count the total number of blocks? (For example, counting "2, 4, 6, 8, 10, 12" for each pair of hexagon-trapezoid.)

   • How many different kinds (or colors) of blocks were used to build the train?

   • How many of each kind of block was used to build the train? (In other words, how many hexagons? How many trapezoids?)

   • (Optional) How many times is the repeating unit, or core, repeated?

   • (Optional) If we make a long train with a core that is repeated 10 times, how many blocks would we need? How many hexagons? How many trapezoids?

7. Have students work independently to complete the activity, *Pattern Trains.kia*. The activity contains nine pattern trains for students to extend and count. Types of repetition include AB, ABC, AAB, ABA, ABB and AABB patterns.

8. Conclude the lesson by discussing all or a selection of the pattern trains. Show a completed activity or have students present their work. For each pattern, include the discussion questions from step 6. In addition, ask students to compare the trains:

   • Which train or trains required the fewest blocks? How many blocks?

   • Which train or trains required the most blocks? How many blocks?

Note: Some students may solve patterns not by counting shapes or color, but by general features. For example, a student might see the pattern below as "flat mountain, pointy mountain, flat mountain, pointy mountain." Encourage students to share all the different ways they saw the pattern.

✓ Assessment

- Assess students on their completed activities, checking for correct repetition of shapes and accurate counts. See *Pattern Trains Exemplar.kid* from the previously downloaded Zip file for a sample completed activity.

Adaptations

- Modify the activity to include written questions similar to those in step 6. Students can respond in writing using a **Math Text Box** from the **Math palette**.

- Students can add additional pages and create their own pattern trains. In pairs, one student can build the beginning of a pattern and the other can extend it.

- To include more complex patterns, or to have students extend patterns a longer distance, use smaller pattern blocks. Unlock any pattern blocks on the page and use the **Resize Manipulatives** button on the **Bottom** toolbar.

- Require students to record an estimate for the length of each train in blocks before extending the pattern. Students can compare their estimates to the actual count.

- Add more complexity to the activity by including patterns that involve rotation of shapes. Students can use the **Rotate** tools on the **Bottom** toolbar to position blocks into place.

- Require that students mark the repeating unit, or core, using the **Cross-Out Stamp**.

Quick Images with Five and Ten Frames

⭐ **Grade Levels: K-2 (Ages 5-8)**

⭐ **NCTM Principles and Standards for School Mathematics**

- Develops a sense of whole numbers and represents and uses them in flexible ways, including relating, composing and decomposing numbers
- Counts with understanding and recognizes "how many" in sets of objects
- Connects number words and numerals to the quantities they represent, using various physical models and representations
- Understands various meanings of addition and subtraction of whole numbers and the relationship between the two operations
- Develops fluency with basic number combinations for addition and subtraction
- Illustrates general principles and properties of operations, such as commutativity, using specific numbers

Note: *These standards are listed with the permission of the National Council of Teachers of Mathematics (NCTM). NCTM does not endorse the content or validity of these alignments.*

Description

After students acquire cardinality and success with counting, they must develop their number sense by discovering relationships between numbers. Five and ten frames have been shown to help students use landmark numbers and progress towards strategies such as "making tens." They also help students develop an understanding of part-whole relationships through composition and decomposition of numbers, and use spatial relationships to determine "how many" in a set of objects. In this lesson, students will use **Kidspiration Color Tiles™** to complete two different quick image activities with five or ten frames. They will call out the number of tiles that they see on the "quick image" or re-create the image using tiles. With both activities, students will discuss their reasoning to develop initial understandings of number relationships, addition, subtraction and properties of operations. This lesson can be done on an ongoing basis throughout students' progression from five frames to ten frames.

Instructions

The resources for this lesson can be found at the following location: **Kidspiration 3 Teacher menu>Teacher Resources Online>Lesson Plans>Grades K-2 Math>Quick Images with Five and Ten Frames**. Save the Zip file. To get started with the first activity, open an included teacher file, either *Five Frames_Teacher.kia* or *Ten Frames_Teacher.kia*. For the second activity, you will also need to open either *Five Frames_Student.kia* or *Ten Frames_Student.kia*.

Note: Young students should become accustomed to working with five frames and the landmark number of 5 before working with ten frames. This lesson will outline instruction using five frames, but the same process can be used with ten frames.

Quick Image Activity 1

1. The first page of the activity (*Five Frames_Teacher.kia* or *Ten Frames_Teacher.kia*) contains instructions. Explain to students that you are going to show an image for only three seconds and that after the image is shown, they must tell you how many tiles they saw. Use the **Go to Next Page** button on the **Math** toolbar to begin. Show the five frame on page 2 for three seconds, then go to page 3 where the words "What did you see?" appear. Students will know that this is their cue to call out the number of tiles that they saw.

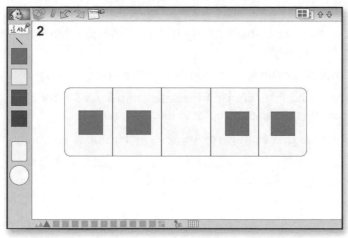

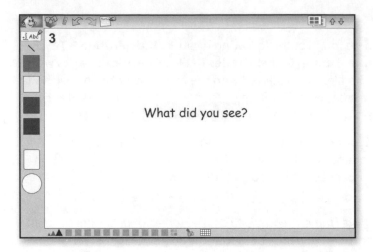

2. After students call out the number of tiles, navigate back to the five frame on page 2 using the **Go to Previous Page** button and ask them to share how they figured this out. Responses will reveal students' understanding about counting, composition and decomposition of numbers, commutativity, addition and subtraction.

For example, after seeing the first five frame, students might answer the question *How did you know there were 4?* in the following way:

- "I saw two groups of 2." (Demonstrates understanding of addition and doubles.)

- "One was blank." (Demonstrates understanding of the relationship between addition and subtraction facts; for example, the relationship between 4+1 and 5-1.)

- "I counted 1, 2, 3, 4." (Demonstrates that students may not have developed recognition of small sets.)

3. Ask students follow-up questions. Options include the following:

- Is this more than 5 or less than 5?

- How many blanks are there?

- How much more do you need to have 5?

- What number sentence could you make for this picture? (Examples: 2+2=4, 5-1=4.)

- Could you have shown the number 4 in a different way? (Tiles can be moved to show other representations.)

4. Go to page 4 and repeat the process for the next image. There are 16 five frames in this activity, each alternating with a "What did you see?" page. Discuss each five frame in depth; student responses will reveal much about their reasoning and also allow students to learn from each other and begin to think about numbers in new ways.

Below are samples of the five frames that students will see, as well as their potential responses:

How did you know there were 3?

- "I saw 1 by itself and a group of 2."
- "I saw a group of 2 and 1 more."

(Take this opportunity to discuss how these two interpretations are the same and different.)

- "I saw 2 blank."
- "I counted 1, 2, 3."

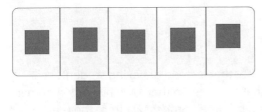

How did you know there were 6?

- "I saw 5 and 1 extra."
- "It was full and then there was also 1 more."

(These two comments demonstrate an understanding of counting on from 5 as opposed to counting each tile from 1.)

- "I counted 1, 2, 3, 4, 5, 6."

Note: Two pages show filled five frames with additional tiles outside of the frame; these are intended to help students transition to using ten frames.

5. If transitioning to ten frames, use *Ten Frames_Teacher.kia* and facilitate the same process of asking students how they determined the number of tiles, and then asking follow-up questions.

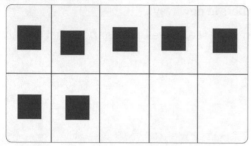

How did you know there were 7?

- "I saw 5 and 2."
- "I saw 2 and 5."
- "There was a full row and 2 more."
- "3 were empty."
- "I saw a group of 4 and 3 more."
- "I saw 2 and 2, and then also 3."

Quick Image Activity 2

This activity is similar to Quick Image Activity 1, except that instead of having students call out how many tiles they saw, they will re-create what they see on their own five or ten frames. Students will use either *Five Frames_Student.kia* or *Ten Frames_Student.kia* from the previously downloaded Zip file. These files include multiple blank five or ten frames to correspond with the number of five or ten frames shown in the teacher file. If necessary, demonstrate how to fill their five or ten frames by bringing out color tiles from the **Math palette**.

With this activity, it's very important that students do not build the image at the same time as it is being shown. Each "What did you see?" page will be their cue to build what they saw. After students have had a chance to re-create the image on their own five or ten frames, ask them what they saw and how they knew what to build.

Assessment

- As students complete Quick Image Activity 2, compare their five or ten frames to the quick image.

- Assess students on their contributions to the discussions about each frame. Do they show an understanding of composition and decomposition of numbers, adding, the relationship between addition and subtraction, counting, and the commutative property?

Adaptations

- Meet the developmental level of your students by increasing or decreasing the number of seconds that each image is shown.

- Ask for the number of spaces on the frame instead of or in addition to the number of tiles.

- Have students call out or build *one more than* or *one less than* the number of tiles shown on the five or ten frame.

- Call five frames and ten frames something else that is meaningful to students. Some teachers prefer to name them "parking lots" or "cubbies."

- Students can use a **Math Text Box** to record corresponding number sentences next to their five or ten frames.

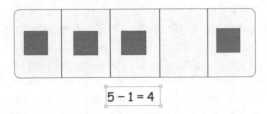

- If completing this activity on a regular basis, begin on a different page each time. Alternatively, mix up the order of the pages or add additional pages through the **Choose Page** dialog.

- To complete Quick Image Activity 2 using one classroom computer, print out blank five or ten frames, enough for one for each student, from *Five Frames_Student.kia* or *Ten Frames_Student.kia*. Have students duplicate what they see using counters, beans, tiles, etc. on their paper five or ten frames.

Composing Shapes

 **Grade Levels: K-5 (Ages 5-11)**

 **NCTM Principles and Standards for School Mathematics**

- Recognizes, names, builds and compares two-dimensional shapes
- Investigates and predicts the results of putting together and taking apart two-dimensional shapes
- Recognizes and represents shapes from different perspectives
- Identifies, compares and analyzes attributes of two-dimensional shapes and develops vocabulary to describe the attributes
- Builds geometric objects
- (Optional) Understands attributes such as length, area and size of angle
- (Optional) Explores congruence and similarity

Note: *These standards are listed with the permission of the National Council of Teachers of Mathematics (NCTM). NCTM does not endorse the content or validity of these alignments.*

Description

In this lesson, students will use **Kidspiration Pattern Blocks™** to build, compare, analyze and describe geometric shapes and their attributes. Students will use basic shapes and spatial reasoning to construct other shapes; for example, using a variety of pattern blocks to build triangles of different sizes and orientations. Class discussion will focus on comparing shapes and describing their attributes using geometric vocabulary. The activity includes options and adaptations that span K-5 measurement and geometry standards. For older students, the activity can include or center on concepts of perimeter, area, similarity and/or congruence.

Instructions

1. The resources for this lesson can be found at the following location: **Kidspiration 3 Teacher menu>Teacher Resources Online>Lesson Plans>Grades K-2 Math>Composing Shapes**. Save the Zip file and open the included *Composing Shapes.kia* activity. Complete the first page of the activity together.

2. Review the meaning of *triangle*. Ask students if they can think of a way to build a triangle using pattern blocks. As necessary, demonstrate how to bring pattern blocks onto the workspace from the **Math palette** and how to use the **Rotate** tools on the **Bottom** toolbar. Have students build triangles on the workspace, one at a time. For each construction, students can write their name next to their triangle using a **Math Text Box**. If students are using physical pattern blocks at their desks, they can re-create and share their construction on the Kidspiration Pattern Blocks workspace. Encourage students to build any and all triangles; triangles can be different sizes, made up of different blocks, turned different ways, etc. Students may need to be reminded that building the biggest triangle is not the goal of the activity.

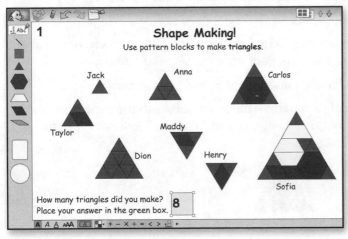

3. Discuss the triangles. The following questions are based on the example above, but the questions can be adjusted to build off of students' work.

   - What do all of these shapes have in common?

   - Which triangle is the smallest? How many blocks did Jack use?

   - Which triangle is the largest? How many blocks did Sofia use?

   - Are there any triangles that are the *same*? How do you know?

   Note: Students may have different definitions of "sameness." For example, some students might claim that Taylor and Anna's triangles are the same because they are the same shape and size. Others might claim that because Taylor and Anna used different blocks, the triangles are different. Encourage this discussion. If students are learning about congruence, then discussion will focus around what makes shapes congruent.

   - What do you notice about Dion and Anna's triangles? Do you think that this will work with other shapes? For example, do you think that you could make big squares out of many little squares? Or big trapezoids out of many little trapezoids, etc.?

   - Were there any pattern block shapes that were *not* used to make triangles?

   - Are there any triangles that seem different than the others? What do you notice about Maddy and Henry's triangles that is different from the rest of the triangles?

   - (Optional) Which triangle(s) has the largest area? How do you know?

   - (Optional) If the side length of each pattern block is 1 unit, with the exception of the trapezoid's base, then what is the perimeter of each triangle? (Perimeters can be recorded next to student names.)

Jack 3

Anna 6

Carlos 9

4. Before students begin working independently, it may be helpful to scroll through all of the pages and review the definition of each shape. Each of the six pages asks students to build different shapes: triangles, trapezoids, hexagons, squares, rectangles and parallelograms.

Notes:

- Certain shapes may not be appropriate depending on the grade level of students and your curriculum. Assign pages as you see fit, or delete pages through the **Choose Page** dialog.

- Students do not need to be familiar with the names of shapes to complete the activity. Modify the activity to include one example for each shape, as below.

Use pattern blocks to make **trapezoids**.

Students can discuss what they notice about the shape. For example, "It has 4 sides," "2 of the sides are parallel, they will never meet," "The other 2 sides are not parallel." Students can then build trapezoids based on the example and the attributes that they identify, without a formal introduction to the shape.

5. Have students work independently or in pairs to complete *Composing Shapes.kia*. Remind students that this is not a race to build the biggest shapes or the most shapes; it is more important to build a *variety* of shapes.

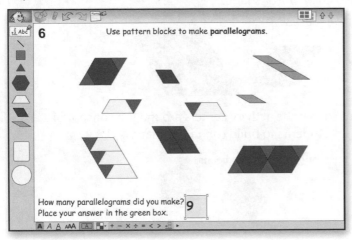

Assessment

- Check completed activities for both the number and variety of constructed shapes. See *Composing Shapes Exemplar.kid* from the previously downloaded Zip file for a sample completed activity.

- Assess students on their participation in class discussions, including their ability to describe attributes of shapes, notice similarities and differences, and use appropriate geometric vocabulary.

Adaptations

- If using one classroom computer, students can use physical pattern blocks to model their shapes. Their representations can be preserved, shared and presented on the Kidspiration Pattern Blocks workspace.

- Modify the instructions so that the activity centers around the concept of similarity, and instruct students to build *similar* shapes.

Use pattern blocks to make <u>similar</u> **parallelograms**.

- Modify the instructions so that the activity centers around the concept of congruence, and instruct students to build *congruent* shapes.

Use pattern blocks to make <u>congruent</u> **hexagons**.

- To structure time, specify a minimum or maximum number of shapes that students should build per page.

- If students need more space, use smaller pattern blocks. Younger students may benefit from manipulating larger pattern blocks. Pattern blocks can be made larger or smaller by using the **Resize Manipulatives** button on the **Bottom** toolbar.

Adding It Up

✦ **Grade Levels: 1-2 (Ages 6-8)**

✦ **NCTM Principles and Standards for School Mathematics**

- Models situations that involve the addition of whole numbers, using objects, pictures and symbols

- Develops fluency with basic number combinations for addition

- Illustrates general principles and properties of operations, such as commutativity, using specific numbers

- Uses concrete representations to develop an understanding of conventional symbolic notation

- Understands the effects of adding whole numbers

- Uses a variety of methods and tools to compute, including objects, mental computation, and paper and pencil

Note: *These standards are listed with the permission of the National Council of Teachers of Mathematics (NCTM). NCTM does not endorse the content or validity of these alignments.*

Description

Conceptual understanding of addition and fluency with basic addition facts is developed through student interaction with a variety of models and contexts. In this lesson, students will use **Kidspiration Color Tiles™** to find and model all of the different numbers that can be paired to reach a given sum. As they see equivalence through color tile "trains" of equal length, students will explore visually why number pairs can have the same sum while appearing different symbolically, such as 4+2 and 5+1. Understanding the relationships between different sums will help build fluency with basic math facts. Students will also have the opportunity to write sums using symbolic notation, share problem-solving strategies and explore the principle of commutativity.

Instructions

1. Begin the lesson by asking students to list all the ways that they could put four apples into two groups. For each combination, write the corresponding sum. For example, 4+0, 3+1, etc.

2. Go to **Kidspiration Starter>Activities>Math** and open the *Adding it Up.kia* activity.

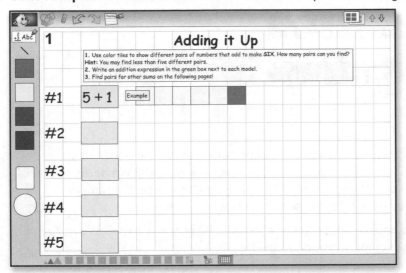

Read the directions aloud, explaining to students that on the first page of the activity, they will find all of the different pairs of numbers that add to make 6. Point to the example, and discuss how tiles in two different colors were used to show the sum, 5+1, and how the corresponding addition expression was recorded in the green box. It may be helpful to ask the students for one additional pair of numbers that add to 6, as this will give you a chance to demonstrate how color tiles can be brought onto the workspace from the **Math palette**, and how the **Plus Sign** can be accessed from the **Bottom** toolbar to write the corresponding sum.

3. Have students work individually or in pairs to complete all four pages of the activity. Students will work with numbers that sum to 6, 8, 5 and 7. Circulate as students are working and note the order in which students pick pairs of numbers. Do they work in a systematic order or do they choose sums randomly? Remind students that they may not be able to find five different pairs, but check to see that they have included the +0 sum, for example, 6+0.

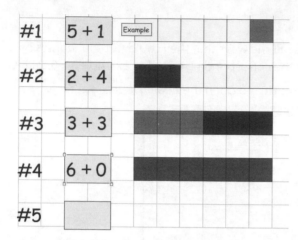

Note: Some students may model two of the same pairs, but in a different order. For example, they may model 1+5 in addition to 5+1. Ask students if this is a different pair of numbers or the same pair in reverse order. If students are modeling the same pair twice, there will be more than five sums to model on each page.

4. After students have completed the activity, conclude the lesson with a class discussion. Include the following prompts in your discussion:

- How did you choose which numbers to add? Did you choose pairs randomly or did you go in a particular order?

- How did you know when you had found all of the pairs for a single sum?

- Did each page have the same number of sums? Which do you think has more sums, 24 or 14. Why?

- Did everyone list the same sums? (Take this opportunity to discuss and illustrate the principle of commutativity. Show visually why two numbers can be added in any order while still reaching the same sum.)

$$2 + 3 = 3 + 2$$

Assessment

- Check completed activities for correct color tile combinations and corresponding symbolic expressions. For a sample completed activity, go to **Kidspiration 3 Teacher menu>Teacher Resources Online>Lesson Plans>Grades K-2 Math>Adding It Up** and open *Adding_It_Up_Exemplar.kid*.

- Pick a number and have students, on paper, find all pairs of numbers that sum to that number. If needed, they can check their work by building models with color tiles.

Adaptations

- If you want students to find *all* pairs for each sum (including those that commute, such as 5+1 and 1+5), provide space by adding additional pages to the activity.

Adding with "Near-Doubles"

Grade Levels: 1-2 (Ages 6-8)

NCTM Principles and Standards for School Mathematics

- Develops and uses strategies for whole number computations, with a focus on addition

- Uses concrete representations to develop an understanding of conventional symbolic notation

- Understands various meanings of addition

- Develops fluency with basic number combinations for addition

- Models situations that involve the addition of whole numbers, using objects, pictures and symbols

Note: These standards are listed with the permission of the National Council of Teachers of Mathematics (NCTM). NCTM does not endorse the content or validity of these alignments.

Description

After students have developed an understanding of the meaning of addition and the contexts in which it is used, they must develop a variety of strategies to compute whole numbers so that they can quickly recall basic facts. Computation strategies such as "counting on," "making tens" or "near-doubles" offer students a variety of methods from which they can select and apply for speed, accuracy and understanding. In this lesson, students will build on their knowledge of "doubles" addition facts by using **Kidspiration Color Tiles™** to learn about the "near-doubles" computation strategy. Through building visual models, they will learn to relate known math facts to unknown math facts, increasing retention while also building conceptual understanding of addition and number relationships beyond rote memorization.

Note: Before beginning this lesson, students should be familiar with doubles addition facts through 10+10. Additionally, they should be able to name numbers that are one more than and one less than any number up to 20.

Instructions

1. Ask two student volunteers to come to the front of the room. Direct the class to look at the two students and tell how many noses they see. What number sentence shows this? (1+1=2) Ask the two volunteers to each raise one hand and put the other hand behind their backs. Now ask how many fingers the class sees, and what number sentence shows this? (5+5=10) How many eyes do they see, and what number sentence shows this? (2+2=4) Repeat as necessary, asking the volunteers to hold up fingers for sums like 3+3, 7+7, etc. When finished, ask students to describe what each of these sums has in common. Remind students that these are called doubles facts, and that knowing doubles facts can help us with more difficult sums.

2. Open a new workspace in the Kidspiration Color Tiles Math Tool. Use a **Math Text Box** to write 4+3. Ask students if they know what 3+3 is, and model it using two rows of color tiles. Is 4+3 more than this, or less than this? How do you know? How many more color tiles need to be added to show 4+3? Add one additional color tile, and explain to students that 4+3 is called a "near-double" because it is close to a doubles fact. In fact we can think of 4+3 as "doubles plus 1." Why? Show students how they can bring out a **Math Text Box** from the **Math palette** and use the buttons on the **Bottom** toolbar to write their number sentence, 3+3+1=7.

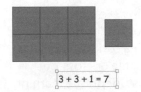

3. Build a second model below the first. Ask students how they might show 4+4 with color tiles. How do the rows of color tiles show that this is a doubles fact? Is 4+3 more than this, or less than this? How do you know? How many more color tiles need to be added or subtracted from the model to show 4+3? Use the **Cross-Out Stamp** to mark one tile and show "taking away." Why can you also think of 4+3 as "doubles minus 1?" Write a second number sentence, 4+4-1=7.

4 + 4 − 1 = 7

Tell students that even if they weren't sure about the answer to 4+3, they could find the answer by thinking about the near doubles that they know, 3+3 and 4+4.

4. Go to **Kidspiration Starter>Activities>Math** and open the *Finding Doubles.kia* activity. Explain to students that they will be working individually and using color tiles to model five different "near doubles" facts. The first page of this activity is an example; discuss the structure of the example and demonstrate how to navigate between pages as necessary.

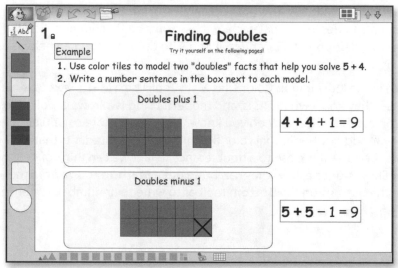

5. Circulate as students are working on *Finding Doubles.kia*. Notice that students are developing an understanding of the computation strategy through a conceptual model in which equal rows clearly show doubles and the additional tile or cross-out shows relationships between addition facts. Through this process, students are learning to identify the smaller addend, double it and add 1 to the sum for "doubles plus 1." For "doubles minus 1," students are learning to identify the larger addend, double it, and subtract 1. However, they are not simply doing this procedurally; they are developing conceptual understanding through the use of the model.

For a sample completed activity, go to **Kidspiration 3 Teacher menu>Teacher Resources Online>Lesson Plans>Grades K-2 Math>Finding Doubles** and open *Finding_Doubles_Exemplar.kid*.

6. After students have finished the activity, have a class discussion that includes the following prompts:

- Did you prefer "doubles plus 1" or "doubles minus 1?" Why?

- How did you decide which doubles facts to use to help you solve the addition problem?

- Could a doubles fact help you solve 6+8? Which doubles fact(s) would help you out? How would you model that?

- How could doubles facts help you solve larger sums, such as 20+21? What about 20+19?

Note: As students work increasingly with larger, multi-digit numbers, their number sense should be developed to the point that they can quickly compute simple sums such as 20+21 without relying on the standard procedure for adding multi-digit numbers. In other words, they are able to think of this as two groups of 20 and 1 more, rather than having to envision their addends aligned vertically before adding the ones and then adding the tens.

Assessment

- Individual students can each present one problem. Assess them on their ability to explain their process, color tiles model and number sentences.

- Check completed activities for correct number sentences and corresponding models.

Adaptations

- Have students add pages to the end of the activity. They can write their own near doubles fact, model it with color tiles and write the corresponding number sentences.

- In addition to modeling doubles in rows, students can also model doubles as equal-sized towers of color tiles.

- Add more pages with additional near-doubles facts. Students can model near-doubles facts with larger addends by using smaller color tiles. Tiles can be resized with the **Resize Manipulatives** button on the **Bottom** toolbar.

- Extend the activity to include facts such as 6+8, where students can use "doubles plus 2" and "doubles minus 2" strategies.

- Students can roll two dice or two number cubes to find sums. They can decide if a near-doubles strategy would be appropriate for the sum that is rolled, and those sums can be modeled with color tiles.

Exploring Place Value

★ **Grade Levels: 1-2 (Ages 6-8)**

★ **NCTM Principles and Standards for School Mathematics**

- Understands the place value structure of the base-ten number system and uses it to represent and compare whole numbers

- Recognizes equivalent representations for the same number and generates them by decomposing and composing numbers

- Connects number words and numerals to the quantities they represent, using various models and representations

Note: These standards are listed with the permission of the National Council of Teachers of Mathematics (NCTM). NCTM does not endorse the content or validity of these alignments.

Description

In this lesson, students will use **Kidspiration Base Ten Blocks™** to model multiple representations of two-digit numbers on a place value mat. As students make connections between equivalent representations, such as modeling 13 with 1 ten and 3 ones or with 13 ones, they will not only learn important place value concepts and develop their number sense, but also build a solid conceptual foundation for later work with regrouping in the base-ten number system. Students will express their answers both visually with a model and numerically in a place value table.

Instructions

1. Open the lesson by telling students that you would like to buy a piece of candy for 17¢. You have a jar of coins and would like help coming up with all of the different ways that you might pay for your candy without needing change back. Encourage students to come up with all possible combinations of pennies, nickels and dimes.

2. Explain to students that they can represent numbers in multiple ways just as they can represent money in multiple ways. Go to **Kidspiration Starter>Activities>Math** and open the *Exploring Place Value.kia* activity.

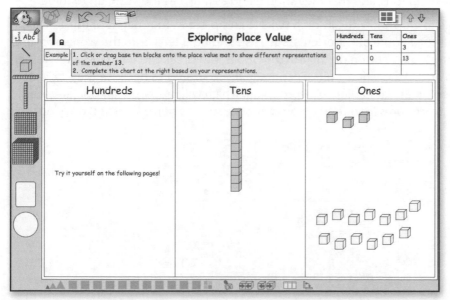

3. The first page of the activity is an example. It may be beneficial to walk through the example from the beginning as a class. If so, the first page of the activity can be unlocked ahead of time from the **Teacher** menu, allowing deletion of base ten blocks and numbers inside the table. Encourage students to think of different ways to represent the number 13. If students are stuck, ask them the following:

   • Can you represent 13 using a flat? If so, how many? If not, why not?

   • Can you represent 13 using a rod? If so, how many? If not, why not?

   • Can you represent 13 using only units? If so, how many? If not, why not?

Demonstrate how to bring blocks onto the place value mat. In addition to showing students how they can drag blocks, also show how they can point to anywhere on the workspace and then click successively on the desired block in the **Math palette**. This will help students bring out large quantities of blocks. Also demonstrate how to distinguish each representation with color and complete the table in the upper-right corner of the workspace to match their representations.

Note: For this activity, there is room in the table for students to record up to three numerical representations. Remind students that there may be more than three or less than three different representations, and that they should find as many as they can, up to three.

4. Allow students to work individually or in pairs to complete all four pages of the activity. Some students may figure out shortcuts, such as bringing 3 tens onto the workspace and using the **Break Apart** button on the **Bottom** toolbar to break them into 30 units, rather than bringing out 30 individual units. Encourage these strategies because they indicate important learning about trading, or regrouping, which will prepare them for later work with efficient procedures for operating on numbers, such as borrowing and carrying.

4
1. Click or drag base ten blocks onto the place value mat to show different representations of the number 30.
2. Complete the chart at the right based on your representations.

Hundreds	Tens	Ones
0	3	0
0	2	10
0	0	30

Hundreds	Tens	Ones

© 2008 Inspiration Software®, Inc.

5. Conclude by showing a completed activity (for a sample, go to **Kidspiration 3 Teacher menu>Teacher Resources Online>Lesson Plans>Grades K-2 Math>Exploring Place Value** and open *Place_Value_Exemplar.kid* or have individual students present their solutions). Discuss the following as a class:

   - How are the representations on each page the same? How are they different?

   - Which representations used the least blocks? If you want to use as few blocks as possible to represent a number, is it better to use as many units as you can or as many rods as you can?

   - Will some numbers have more than three different representations? What is an example?

   - Did you discover any shortcuts while working on the activity?

   - What patterns do you notice in the tables?

Assessment

   - Assess students on their completed activities, checking for the correct number of blocks and correct placement of blocks on the place value mat. Confirm that the information in the table corresponds with each representation.

   - If individual students present their work, assess their ability to communicate their thinking and their process to the class.

Adaptations

   - Add pages to lengthen the activity or add an increasing variety of numbers. Consider including numbers in the hundreds or thousands.

   - Connect this activity to equivalent representations elsewhere in the world. In Picture View, students can use coins from the *Money* Symbol library under *Math & Numbers* to show multiple representations of dollar amounts. For an example, see *Making Change.kia* located here: **Kidspiration Starter>Activities>Math**.

Fact Families for Addition and Subtraction

✦ **Grade Levels: 1-2 (Ages 6-8)**

✦ **NCTM Principles and Standards for School Mathematics**

- Understands various meanings of addition and subtraction and the relationship between the two operations

- Models situations that involve the addition and subtraction of whole numbers, using objects, pictures, and symbols

- Develops fluency with basic number combinations for addition and subtraction

- Illustrates general principles and properties of operations, such as commutativity, using specific numbers

- Develops and uses strategies for whole number computations, with a focus on addition and subtraction

- Uses concrete representations to develop an understanding of conventional symbolic notation

- Develops a sense of whole numbers and represents and uses them in flexible ways, including relating, composing, and decomposing numbers

Note: These standards are listed with the permission of the National Council of Teachers of Mathematics (NCTM). NCTM does not endorse the content or validity of these alignments.

Description

Recognizing and understanding the inverse relationship between addition and subtraction is critical to students' development of number sense and their ability to flexibly use both operations to solve problems. In this lesson, students will use **Kidspiration Color Tiles™** to build tile trains and model fact families for addition and subtraction. Using color and cross-outs to represent "adding" and "taking away," students will make connections between composition, decomposition, the commutative property, and the related operations of addition and subtraction. Students will also write number sentences that correspond to their fact family models.

Instructions

1. Go to **Kidspiration Starter>Activities>Math** and open the *Fact Families.kia* activity. The first page of the activity is an example with the fact family numbers 3, 8 and 5.

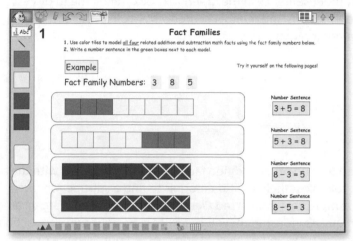

2. Students may benefit from going through the example from start to finish. If so, unlock the page ahead of time from the **Teacher** menu, delete all of the color tiles and number sentences, and complete the problem as a class.

   Read the fact family numbers aloud and ask students how they might use color tiles to show an addition fact involving all three numbers. For example, will a color tile train of 3 tiles and 8 tiles have a total length of 5? Model different scenarios as necessary, until students recognize that the larger number, 8, needs to be the total length. If students choose to show 3+5 first, have them describe how they could show the sum with color tiles. Demonstrate how to bring color tiles, in two colors, from the **Math palette** into the first **Math SuperGrouper™** to build their train. Discuss what each color represents and emphasize that it does not matter what colors they choose, as long as their train clearly shows a group of 3 and a group of 5. Demonstrate how to click inside the green text box and use math symbols from the **Bottom** toolbar to record the corresponding number sentence.

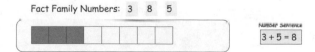

Ask students if they can think of another addition fact using the numbers 3, 5 and 8. Does it matter if the group of 3 comes first? Will the train still have 8 tiles if the 5 comes before the 3? How can they prove this? Have a student volunteer use color tiles to model the second addition fact and record the number sentence in the green text box. Take time to discuss how the first and second representations and number sentences are alike and different. What does this tell them about adding two numbers?

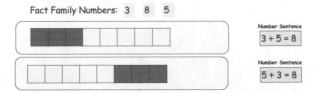

4. After students have determined that no other addition facts can be represented with the fact family numbers, ask them to look at their addition models to find a subtraction fact. Students may recognize, for example, that if the 3 red tiles that formed the train are taken away, the 5 yellow tiles will remain. Ask for student volunteers to represent two subtraction facts with tiles, demonstrating how tiles can be selected and crossed out with the **Cross-Out Stamp** to show "taking away."

Note: Students may choose to model the subtraction facts in different ways. Encourage them to use whichever model best helps them to see the relationship between addition and subtraction.

For example, a student might use the same color combinations as their addition models, demonstrating the relationship between the composed numbers in addition and the decomposed numbers in subtraction.

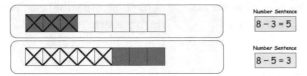

Other students may choose to use a single color and apply cross-outs from either the right or the left.

5. Once all four addition and subtraction facts have been represented, discuss the relationship between the four models. How are the subtraction trains similar to the addition trains? Help students make the connection between the composed quantities in the addition trains and the decomposed quantities in the subtraction trains, using language like "parts" and "total." How are the number sentences the same and different?

6. Have students work independently or in pairs to complete models for three different fact families in the activity *Fact Families.kia*. All fact family sums are 10 or under. While students are working and after they have finished, focus the conversation on the relationship between addition and subtraction and how the composed and decomposed tiles show properties of operations.

Assessment

- Give students a number, then have them think of two other numbers and write all related addition and subtraction facts in the fact family.

- Check activities for completion, appropriate color tile models, and correct sums and differences. For a sample completed activity, go to **Kidspiration 3 Teacher menu>Teacher Resources Online>Lesson Plans>Grades K-2 Math>Fact Families for Addition and Subtraction** and open *Fact_Families_Exemplar.kid*.

Adaptations

- Add pages to include different fact family numbers. To represent larger quantities with smaller color tiles, use the **Resize Manipulatives** button on the **Bottom** toolbar.

- Modify the activity so that the green text boxes contain the number sentences. Students can focus on modeling the sums and differences with color tiles.

- Students can add pages to the activity and model their own fact family sums and differences. In pairs, one student can come up with the fact family numbers and the other student can model the related addition and subtraction facts.

Covering Hexagons

✦ **Grade Levels: 1-3 (Ages 6-9)**

✦ **NCTM Principles and Standards for School Mathematics**

- Recognizes, names, builds and compares two-dimensional shapes
- Investigates and predicts the results of putting together two-dimensional shapes
- Relates ideas in geometry to ideas in number and measurement
- Models problems with objects and uses tables to draw conclusions
- Explores congruence

Note: These standards are listed with the permission of the National Council of Teachers of Mathematics (NCTM). NCTM does not endorse the content or validity of these alignments.

Description

In this activity, students will use **Kidspiration Pattern Blocks™** to compose shapes in the context of dressing snowmen. They will build spatial reasoning and problem-solving skills by finding different combinations, arrangements and orientations of shapes that form hexagons, thereby developing an understanding of congruence. Students will name and compare shapes and also explore the concept of equivalence by working informally with halves, thirds and sixths. After building their snowmen, they will count and record their solutions in a table.

Instructions

1. Open a new workspace in the Kidspiration Pattern Blocks Math Tool. From the **Math palette**, bring a blue hexagon onto the workspace. Ask students if they can find a way to cover the hexagon using exactly two more blocks, and then have one or more students show their solution on the classroom computer. Demonstrate how to use the **Rotate** tools on the **Bottom** toolbar to position blocks as necessary. It may be helpful if students have physical pattern blocks with which they can experiment before representing their answer using Kidspiration Pattern Blocks.

2. Ask students to find other ways to cover the hexagon using three blocks and then four blocks, showing their solutions and discussing any differences in the arrangement of blocks. Encourage students to name each shape when describing their arrangements.

3. The resources for the student activity portion of this lesson can be found at the following location: **Kidspiration 3 Teacher menu>Teacher Resources Online>Lesson Plans>Grades K-2 Math>Covering Hexagons**. Save the Zip file and open the included *Covering Hexagons.kia* activity. Explain to students that they will be "dressing" the snowmen with pattern blocks. Each of the nine snowman sections, or hexagons, must look different.

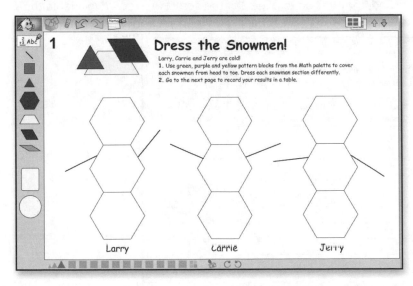

4. Have students work independently or in pairs to complete the activity. Allow students to openly explore composing shapes to cover the hexagon in nine different ways. Students will find different combinations of blocks (for example, using two rhombuses and two triangles) and different orderings (for example, placing the two rhombuses side-by-side or separating them with the two triangles). The following represents eight different ways to compose patterns blocks to form a hexagon. However, because students can also orient their blocks in multiple ways (for example, two trapezoids can be oriented one on top of the other or side-by-side), this opens up many more possibilities for the snowmen to "look" different.

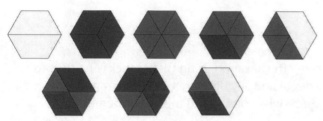

Note: It is not important that students understand and use the terms "arrangement," "ordering" or "orientation," but rather that they are actively engaged in the process of composing shapes to form hexagons. See *Covering Hexagons Exemplar.kid* from the previously downloaded Zip file for a sample completed activity.

5. When students are finished, they will go to page 2 of the activity to record in a table the number and type of each block used to dress their snowman sections.

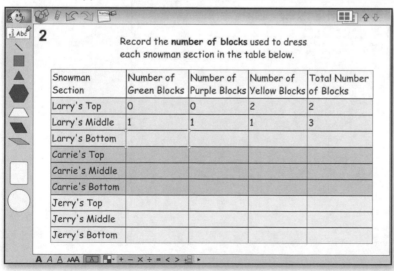

Record the **number of blocks** used to dress each snowman section in the table below.

Snowman Section	Number of Green Blocks	Number of Purple Blocks	Number of Yellow Blocks	Total Number of Blocks
Larry's Top	0	0	2	2
Larry's Middle	1	1	1	3
Larry's Bottom				
Carrie's Top				
Carrie's Middle				
Carrie's Bottom				
Jerry's Top				
Jerry's Middle				
Jerry's Bottom				

6. Ask several students to present their snowmen to the class and engage students in talking about their designs. Include the following in the discussion:

    - What was the greatest number of blocks used for a section of a snowman? Which blocks were used?

    - What was the least number of blocks used for a section of a snowman? Which blocks were used?

    - What strategies were used to find different ways to dress the snowmen? Did anyone have a systematic approach?

    - What are some examples of trades that you could make? For instance, if you took out a yellow block, what could you replace it with to make a snowman section look different?

7. (Optional) Make a class table that combines the information from individual student tables. Discuss any noticeable patterns.

Assessment

- Confirm that students have completed the activity as instructed, and that their table contains accurate sums.

- Assess students on their participation in the class discussion. How did they describe their approach? Did they understand the concept of trading blocks to fill equivalent amounts of space?

Adaptations

- Add more structure to the activity by requiring specific blocks on each snowman. For example, require that Larry wear at least one yellow block on each section, require that Carrie wear at least one purple block on each section, etc.

- Add more pages to the document to build other designs containing hexagons that students must cover with blocks.

Regrouping Game

★ **Grade Levels: 1-3 (Ages 6-9)**

★ **NCTM Principles and Standards for School Mathematics**

- Develops and uses strategies for whole number computations

- Understands the effects of subtracting whole numbers

- Recognizes equivalent representations for the same number and generates them by decomposing and composing numbers

- Uses a variety of methods and tools to compute, including objects and pencil and paper

- Understands the place value structure of the base-ten number system

Note: *These standards are listed with the permission of the National Council of Teachers of Mathematics (NCTM). NCTM does not endorse the content or validity of these alignments.*

Description

In this lesson, students will use **Kidspiration Base Ten Blocks™** to play a game in pairs that helps them understand regrouping in the context of subtracting numbers. They will roll number cubes to determine the number of units to remove from the place value mat, thereby sharpening their basic addition facts, and then regroup as necessary to subtract the units. Students will also record each subtraction fact, strengthening the relationship between the visual model and the numbers and operation that it represents.

Instructions

1. The "game board" for this lesson can be found at the following location: **Kidspiration 3 Teacher menu>Teacher Resources Online>Lesson Plans>Grades K-2 Math>Regrouping Game**. Open the *Regrouping_Game.kia* activity. Explain to students that they will be playing a game with a partner and that they will be competing to clear the base ten blocks off of the place value mat. Show the game board and review as necessary the value of each block and its place on the mat. Ask students the total value represented by base ten blocks.

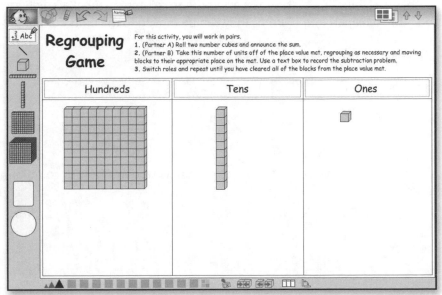

2. Ask for a student volunteer who will be your partner while demonstrating the game. Your partner (the student volunteer) will roll two number cubes and announce the sum. Your job is to take that number of units off of the place value mat. For example, if the student rolls a 4 and a 3, they would announce the sum of 7 and now you must to take 7 units away from 111. Ask students how you might take 7 units away since there is just 1 unit on the place value mat. Elicit students' descriptions as to how they might regroup, or exchange one rod for 10 units. Demonstrate how to use the **Break Apart** button on the **Bottom** toolbar to make exchanges.

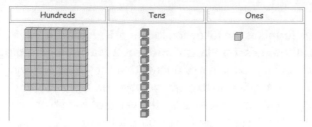

Remind students that each block must stay in its appropriate column on the place value mat. After the rod is broken apart into 10 units, they can be moved to the units column.

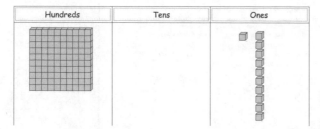

Now you are able to take away seven units from the mat. Show students how to count and delete seven blocks.

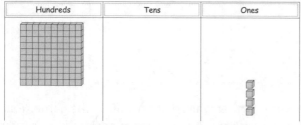

3. Record the subtraction fact that corresponds to the round just completed, such as 111-7 = 104. Switch roles and complete another round, continuing the demonstration until students have seen that some rounds will involve regrouping, or making exchanges, while other rounds will not. Some rounds will involve clearing both rods and units from the mat, and others only units. Explain to students that the partner that takes the last blocks off of the place value mat wins the game. To clear the mat, the last roll must be greater than or equal to the quantity left on the mat.

4. Break students into pairs to complete the activity. Students can play the game as many times as necessary to give them sufficient practice with regrouping and subtraction.

5. After all pairs have completed at least two games, discuss the game as a class. Include the following in your discussion:

   • What was the greatest number of blocks that you were able to remove from the mat at once? Do you think that in this game you could ever remove more than that? What is the largest sum possible when rolling two number cubes?

   • What was the least number of blocks that you were able to remove from the mat at once? Do you think that in this game you could ever remove less than that? What is the smallest sum possible when rolling two number cubes?

   • Did you always have to trade one kind of block for other blocks? What kinds of trades did you make? When did this happen?

   • How did you clear the mat at the end of the game?

Assessment

   • Evaluate students on their participation in both class and pair discussions. Determine if students understand when, why and how to regroup.

   • Check for accuracy in the list of subtraction facts that students complete while playing the game.

Adaptations

   • To focus solely on regrouping between ones and tens, change the initial representation to a two-digit number, such as 74. Use one number cube to determine the number of units that should be removed from the mat.

   • For an added challenge, use a four column place value mat and work with the thousands blocks as well. Students can use three or more number cubes to determine the number of units to remove from the mat.

Growing Patterns

★ **Grade Levels: 1-4 (Ages 6-10)**

★ **NCTM Principles and Standards for School Mathematics**

- Analyzes how growing patterns are generated
- Describes change qualitatively and quantitatively
- Recognizes, names and builds with two-dimensional shapes
- Understand situations that entail addition and multiplication
- Describes, extends and makes generalizations about geometric and numeric patterns
- Investigates how a change in one variable relates to change in a second variable
- Represents and analyzes patterns using words, symbolic notation and tables

Note: These standards are listed with the permission of the National Council of Teachers of Mathematics (NCTM). NCTM does not endorse the content or validity of these alignments.

Description

Elementary students are accustomed to working with repeating patterns in and out of math, including patterns involving repetition of colors, words or motions. While work with repeating patterns gives students a lot of practice predicting what comes next, they have fewer opportunities to work with growing patterns, the foundation of algebraic thinking. In this activity, students use **Kidspiration Pattern Blocks™** to build and extend growing patterns, describe these patterns visually and numerically, and use patterns to make predictions. They will make connections between the many ways that growing patterns can be described—with words, numbers, tables and visual models.

Instructions

1. The resources for this lesson can be found at the following location: **Kidspiration 3 Teacher menu>Teacher Resources Online>Lesson Plans>Grades K-2 Math>Growing Patterns**. Save the Zip file and open the included *Growing Patterns.kia* activity. Explain to students that they will be using pattern blocks to build animals and objects that grow.

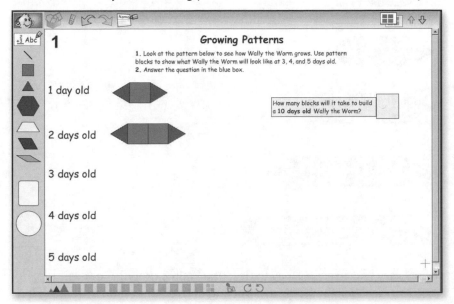

2. Complete page 1 of the activity together. Begin by asking students how the 1-day-old Wally the Worm is alike and different from the 2-day-old Wally the Worm. Which part of Wally is growing and how is it growing? Encourage a variety of explanations and precise descriptions. Some students may struggle to verbalize how Wally is changing, but will have little difficulty building Wally at days 3, 4 and 5.

3. Ask for student volunteers to build Wally at days 3, 4 and 5 based on the pattern. You may choose to demonstrate how the **Cross-Out Stamp** on the **Bottom** toolbar can be used to show what has been changed or added in each design.

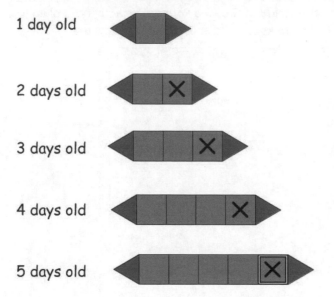

1 day old

2 days old

3 days old

4 days old

5 days old

Note: Some students may find a second way to describe Wally's growth. For example, from day 1 to day 2, they may see Wally's middle as doubling in size rather than increasing by one. In this case, the 3-day-old Wally would have four red squares and the 4-day-old Wally would have eight red squares, etc. Encourage students to find multiple growth patterns.

4. Ask students to determine, without using pattern blocks, the number of blocks it would take to build the 6-day-old Wally. Then work together to answer the question in the blue **Math Text Box** about the number of blocks required to build the 10-day-old Wally. Encourage students to justify their answer with a general rule, such as "the number of days is the same as the number of red squares in the middle, and then he has a head and a tail." Students will see that they can determine the number of blocks used on the 10th day by adding 10+2, thus finding a numerical rule as well.

5. Have students work independently to complete all six pages of the activity, each of which contains a different growth pattern. While circulating, encourage students to describe their patterns with both words and numbers.

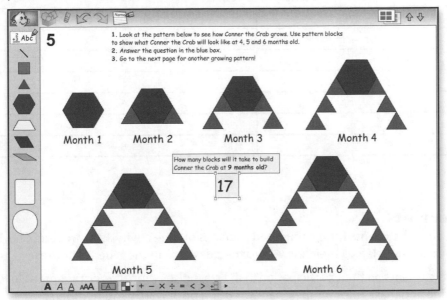

6. Conclude by showing a completed activity (see *Growing Patterns Exemplar.kid* from the previously downloaded Zip file for a sample completed activity or have individual students present their solutions). For each growing pattern, ask students the following:

   • How can this growing pattern be described in words?

   • What is a general rule for determining how many blocks a design will contain when simply given the number of days (or months, years, etc.)?

   • What numbers helped you find the answer to the question in the blue box?

   • Is there more than one way that this pattern can grow?

   • What similarities do you notice between patterns? Is Wally on page 1 growing in the same way as the streetlights on page 3? Discuss how patterns might differ visually while still growing similarly numerically.

7. For at least two of the patterns, create a table as a class that corresponds with each growing pattern. Discuss any noticeable numerical patterns, and connect these to the visual model.

Wally the Worm

Number of Days	Total Number of Blocks
1	3
2	4
3	5
4	6
5	7
6	8

Assessment

- Confirm that students have completed all pages of the activity as instructed. Check their visual models and their answers to the questions in the blue text boxes.

- Assess students on their participation in the class discussion. Were students able to describe and make rules for their patterns using both words and numbers?

Adaptations

- For each pattern, challenge students to find more than one way that it can grow.

- Students can add pages to the activity and make their own growing designs using pattern blocks.

- Use pattern blocks to show a shrinking pattern and have students extend the pattern and describe it with words and numbers.

- Older students can write equations to describe growth, such as B=2+D, where B stands for "number of blocks" and D stands for "age in days."

Multi-Digit Addition

★ **Grade Levels: 2-3 (Ages 7-9)**

★ **NCTM Principles and Standards for School Mathematics**

- Models situations that involve the addition of whole numbers, using objects, pictures and symbols

- Recognizes equivalent representations for the same number and generates them by decomposing and composing numbers

- Uses a variety of methods and tools to compute, including objects, mental computation, estimation, and pencil and paper

- Develops and uses strategies for whole number computations

- Understands the place value structure of the base-ten number system

Note: These standards are listed with the permission of the National Council of Teachers of Mathematics (NCTM). NCTM does not endorse the content or validity of these alignments.

Description

Elementary school students must develop fluency with efficient procedures for adding and subtracting multi-digit numbers, and understand such procedures in the context of place value. Students often learn the process of "carrying" and "borrowing" by rote, without tying it to important place value concepts. In this lesson, students will use **Kidspiration Base Ten Blocks™** to solve multi-digit addition problems using visual models. After completing the activity, they will translate the steps that they take with base ten blocks to a standard procedure for adding multi-digit numbers.

Note: This lesson outlines the process for connecting work with base ten blocks to the traditional algorithm for adding multi-digit numbers. However, the activity can also be used if your curriculum has students develop their own strategies for adding multi-digit numbers, or introduces students to another method, such as the partial sums method. Whichever procedure or method is used, this lesson supports students' understanding of the underlying place value concepts. The lesson can serve as an introduction to a procedure for adding multi-digit numbers, or to reinforce conceptual understanding among students who have already learned a procedure.

Instructions

1. Open a new workspace in the Kidspiration Base Ten Blocks Math Tool. On the **Bottom** toolbar, click the **Place Value Mat** button three times to add a four-column place value mat to the workspace. Explain to students that they are going to use base ten blocks to help them add large numbers. Bring out a **Math Text Box** from the **Math palette** and use the **Open Frame** and **Plus Sign** buttons on the **Bottom** toolbar to write the problem 1136+297.

2. Ask students to estimate the sum, and then elicit suggestions for representing the first addend, 1136, with base ten blocks. From the **Math palette**, bring out 1 thousand, 1 hundred, 3 tens and 6 ones. Ask students how they might represent the second addend, 297. After bringing the blocks out, distinguish them from the first addend by changing their color using a **Color** button on the **Bottom** toolbar.

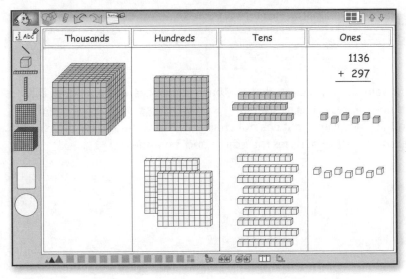

3. Have students count the ones. Is 13 ones the only way to represent this quantity, or can we regroup? Select 10 ones and use the **Group** button on the **Bottom** toolbar to exchange the 10 ones for 1 ten.

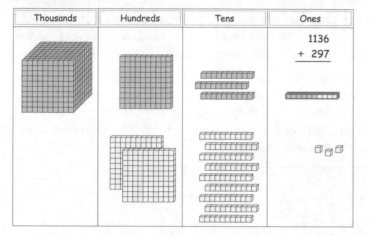

Thousands	Hundreds	Tens	Ones

Ask the class if the total value, as represented by the base ten blocks, has changed. Discuss how the quantity 13 is now represented as 1 ten and 3 ones instead of 13 ones, but the value of the blocks on the place value mat has not changed. It may help to remind students that this is very similar to trading 13 pennies for 1 dime and 3 pennies.

4. Ask students where on the place value mat this new ten should live. Move it to the tens column and have students count the number of tens.

Thousands	Hundreds	Tens	Ones
			1136 + 297

5. Once students determine that they can regroup the tens, select 10 tens and use the **Group** button to exchange them for 1 hundred.

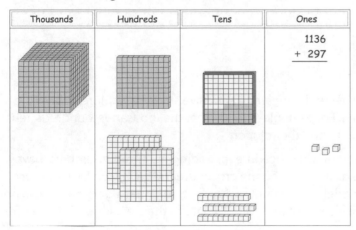

Thousands	Hundreds	Tens	Ones
			1136 + 297

6. Ask students again if the value of blocks changed when regrouping occurred. Make sure that students are able to vocalize that there were 13 tens and now there is 1 hundred and 3 tens, and that these quantities are the same. The notion that only the representation, or make-up, has changed, and not the quantity, is critical to students understanding conceptually what goes on when adding multi-digit numbers using the standard procedure.

7. Move the new hundred to the hundreds column and ask students to count the hundreds. Can we regroup? Why not? How many thousands are there? What is the total value of the blocks now that we have added 1136 and 297? Use a **Math Text Box** to record the answer of 1433.

Thousands	Hundreds	Tens	Ones
			1136 + 297

Note: For steps 3-7, you may wish to demonstrate and have students explore adding the place-values in a different order. For example, adding all of the thousands, hundreds, tens and ones, and then regrouping to find the solution.

8. If students are familiar with a standard procedure for adding multi-digit numbers, have a volunteer complete the same problem using the procedure. Tie each step in their process to each step with the visual model. For example, with the traditional algorithm below, how does writing a 3 in the ones place and "carrying" a 1 relate to the exchange of 13 ones for 1 ten and 3 ones?

© 2008 Inspiration Software®, Inc.

If students have not been introduced to a standard procedure, wait until they finish the student activity portion of the lesson before developing the procedure and tying it to the visual model.

9. The resources for the student activity portion of this lesson can be found at the following location: **Kidspiration 3 Teacher menu>Teacher Resources Online>Lesson Plans>Grades K-2 Math>Multi-Digit Addition.** Save the Zip file and open the included *Multi-Digit Addition.kia* activity. Students will complete six addition problems that are similar to the example problem. Circulate while students are working and ask them to verbalize their reasoning as they perform each step.

10. Reconvene as a class and go over each problem. Individual students or pairs can present one problem each.

Assessment

- Check completed activities for correct sums and use of regrouping. See *Addition Exemplar.kid* from the previously downloaded Zip file for a sample completed activity.

- Assess students on their ability to communicate their thinking and their process during the class example, independent work, and presentations.

- Give students a multi-digit addition problem and have them solve it using both base ten blocks and a paper-pencil procedure.

Adaptations

- As necessary, modify the column headings on the place value mats to fit your curriculum. For example, the headings *Ones, Tens, Hundreds and Thousands* can be changed to *Units, Rods, Flats and Blocks.*

- The activity *Multi-Digit Addition.kia* has students work with numbers through the thousands and contains problems that require regrouping up to three times. For work with smaller addends and problems requiring regrouping only once, see *Adding with Regrouping.kia* located here: **Kidspiration Starter>Activities>Math**.

Subtraction with Regrouping

✦ **Grade Levels: 2-3 (Ages 7-9)**

✦ **NCTM Principles and Standards for School Mathematics**

- Develops and uses strategies for whole number computations

- Recognizes equivalent representations for the same number and generates them by decomposing and composing numbers

- Uses a variety of methods and tools to compute, including objects and pencil and paper

- Develops fluency in subtracting whole numbers

- Understands the place value structure of the base-ten number system

Note: These standards are listed with the permission of the National Council of Teachers of Mathematics (NCTM). NCTM does not endorse the content or validity of these alignments.

Description

Students often memorize procedures for working with multi-digit numbers, such as "carrying" and "borrowing," without a conceptual understanding of such procedures in the context of place value. In this lesson, students will work with **Kidspiration Base Ten Blocks™** to solve multi-digit subtraction problems with visual models. After students have had concrete experiences with regrouping and place value models, they will discuss and translate their models to an efficient procedure for subtracting multi-digit numbers.

Note: This lesson outlines a process for using base ten blocks so that students can connect their work to regrouping algorithms for subtracting multi-digit numbers. However, the activity can also be used if your curriculum has students develop their own strategies for subtracting multi-digit numbers, or introduces students to another method. Whichever procedure or method is used, this lesson supports students' understanding of the underlying place value concepts. The lesson can serve as an introduction to a procedure or to reinforce conceptual understanding among students who have already learned a procedure.

Instructions

1. Open a new workspace in the Kidspiration Pattern Blocks Math Tool. Click the **Place Value Mat** button on the **Bottom** toolbar twice to add the mat shown in the example below to the workspace, and use a **Math Text Box** to write a 3-digit subtraction problem that does not require regrouping, such as 145-24. Ask students to describe the first step in modeling this problem. Bring out base ten blocks from the **Math palette** to represent 145, demonstrating as necessary that blocks can be brought out by dragging or by clicking successively. Ask students to describe how they would subtract 24. Demonstrate how to use the **Cross-Out Stamp** on the **Bottom** toolbar to show "taking away" 2 tens and 4 ones visually. Record the answer in another text box.

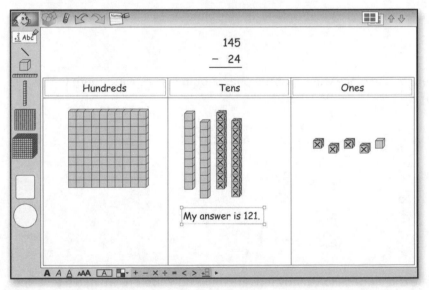

2. Add a second page to the document, this time setting up a subtraction problem that requires regrouping, such as 145-28. Ask students to estimate the difference.

Students may suggest that they are able to take away 2 tens from 4 tens, but unable to take away 8 ones from 5 ones. Ask students how they might get enough ones to be able to take away 8 ones. Facilitate a discussion about regrouping, or borrowing from the tens. Model how to select a ten and use the **Break Apart** button on the **Bottom** toolbar to regroup the ten for 10 ones.

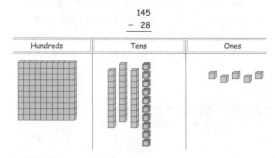

3. Ask students where on the place value mat the ones should live, moving them to the appropriate column.

How many ones are there now? How many tens are there now? Before we had 4 tens and 5 ones, and now we have 3 tens and 15 ones. Have students count and add the blocks to determine if the total value, 145, has changed. Emphasize that a trade has been made, and while there is now a different combination of blocks, the quantity remains the same.

4. Do we have enough to take away 8 ones? Use the **Cross-Out Stamp** to show taking away 8 ones. Do we have enough tens to take away 2 tens? Cross off 2 tens as well.

$$145$$
$$-\ 28$$

Hundreds	Tens	Ones

Have students count how many hundreds, tens and ones remain to determine the final answer of 117 and compare it to their estimate. Compare the subtraction problem on page 1 with the problem on page 2. How are these problems different? How are they the same? Why did one problem involve regrouping while the other did not?

5. (Optional) Complete both problems on the board or overhead projector without using manipulatives. If students are familiar with a standard procedure for subtracting multi-digit numbers, discuss the relationship between each step of the procedure and the model that they just used. For example, using the traditional algorithm, how does crossing out the 4 in the tens place, writing a 3, and then changing the 5 in the ones place to 15, relate to their model with base ten blocks?

6. Go to **Kidspiration Starter>Activities>Math** and open the *Subtraction with Regrouping.kia* activity. Explain to students that they will be working on this activity, and that the first page is an example. If necessary, demonstrate how to navigate between pages.

7. Reconvene as a class and go over each problem in the activity, paying special attention to the order in which steps are taken and when and why regrouping does or does not occur. Does regrouping always occur with ones and tens, or can it occur in other columns? Once students have enough experience with regrouping and using concrete place value models, facilitate the development of an efficient procedure for subtracting multi-digit numbers.

Assessment

- Assess students' process and accuracy during independent work, as well as their contributions to the initial problem and class discussions.

- Activities can be assessed for completion and correctness, paying careful attention to correct use of regrouping and a thorough explanation of steps taken. For a sample completed activity, go to **Kidspiration 3 Teacher menu>Teacher Resources Online>Lesson Plans>Grades K-2 Math>Subtraction with Regrouping** and open *Subtract_Regroup_Exemplar.kid*.

- Individual students can present their solutions to the three problems. Presenters can be assessed on the accuracy of their solution and the description of their process to the class.

Adaptations

- *Subtraction with Regrouping.kia* can also be used to help students develop mental math strategies for subtracting numbers. For example, to represent 145-28, they could subtract 30 (cross off 3 tens) and then add 2 ones.

- For each problem in the activity *Subtraction with Regrouping.kia*, students must regroup once, either between tens and ones or hundreds and tens. Increase the level of difficulty by adding and interspersing pages containing problems that require regrouping twice and problems that do not require any regrouping. Include problems with thousands by choosing a four-column place value mat.

- Delete the blocks on each page of the activity, requiring students to represent the minuend (initial value) with blocks before beginning the subtraction problem.

- If the activity is used as a starting point for learning a procedure for subtracting multi-digit numbers, facilitate a discussion in which students begin to develop their own procedures after working with the visual models.

- If students need more practice subtracting without regrouping prior to beginning this lesson, complete the activity *Subtraction with Blocks.kia* located here: **Kidspiration Starter>Activities>Math**.

Comparing Areas

 **Grade Levels: 2-5 (Ages 7-11)**

 **NCTM Principles and Standards for School Mathematics**

- Recognizes the attribute of area and compares and orders objects accordingly
- Understands how to measure using nonstandard units
- Recognizes geometric ideas and relationships and applies them to problems that arise in the classroom
- Develops strategies for finding areas of irregular shapes

Note: *These standards are listed with the permission of the National Council of Teachers of Mathematics (NCTM). NCTM does not endorse the content or validity of these alignments.*

Description

In this activity, students will use **Kidspiration Pattern Blocks™** to compare areas of non-standard shapes. While deepening their understanding of area as a measurable attribute, they will develop and use a variety of strategies for problem-solving, including finding a common unit of area measurement and finding equivalencies among shapes to determine relative size. Students will discuss, write about and present their solutions.

Instructions

1. Open a new workspace in the Kidspiration Pattern Blocks Math Tool. From the **Math palette**, bring pattern blocks onto the workspace to create the following shapes. Demonstrate how to use the **Rotate** tools on the **Bottom** toolbar to position blocks as necessary.

2. Ask students which shape has a greater area and why. Students may need to be reminded that area refers to the space inside of a shape. Some might automatically assume that because a shape is elongated or taller, it has a larger area. Ask students to justify their choice, and encourage all approaches to solving this problem.

Students might propose that since one purple rhombus is equivalent to two green triangles, the first shape can be thought of as composed of five green triangles, and the second shape as composed of four green triangles. By taking this approach, students are finding a common unit of area measurement, the triangle, to make comparisons. You might choose to show how overlapping shapes can help students use a common unit of measurement.

5 green triangles   4 green triangles

Other students might work backwards and match blocks in each shape. For example, both shapes contain one purple block and one green block. Of the remaining blocks, there is a purple block in the first shape and a green block in the second shape, the latter of which is smaller. Using the **Cross-Out Stamp** on the **Bottom** toolbar can help students visualize matches for those who choose to solve the problem this way.

The first shape is larger by half of a purple rhombus, or 1 green triangle.

Use **Math Text Boxes** to write descriptions for any of the strategies developed. After listening to a variety of approaches, reach a consensus as a class that the first shape has a greater area than the second shape.

3. The resources for the student activity portion of this lesson can be found at the following location: **Kidspiration 3 Teacher menu>Teacher Resources Online>Lesson Plans>Grades 3-5 Math>Comparing Areas**. Save the Zip file and open the included *Comparing Areas.kia* activity. Explain to students that they will use pattern blocks to compare the areas of the two creatures. Remind students that there are a variety of strategies they could use to compare the creatures. For each comparison, students must write about which creature is bigger and why in the yellow text box.

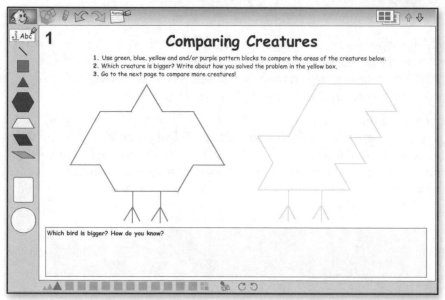

4. Have students work independently or in pairs to complete the activity. Some students might choose to fill the outlines with different blocks and then compare the two sets of blocks, looking for equivalencies. Other students might use a common unit of measurement, such as a triangle or rhombus. Others might fill both creatures simultaneously by, for example, filling each outline with two hexagons, and then one rhombus each, etc. There are three pages in this activity, so you may require that students use a different method of comparison on each page. See *Comparing Areas Exemplar.kid* from the previously downloaded Zip file for a sample completed activity.

5. Conclude the activity by sharing student work and discussing the variety of approaches taken by students. Include the following in your discussion:

   • Were any approaches more correct than others?

   • When comparing areas, what equivalencies did you notice (for example, one hexagon is equivalent in area to six triangles, etc.)? What other equivalencies have we learned about when working with money, time or length?

   • Do shapes with bigger areas also have more sides? Compare the creatures on page 2, which have the same area but a different number of sides.

   • Was there a common unit of measurement that worked best? Why did the triangle work better than the rhombus?

Assessment

   • Confirm that students have completed all pages of the activity, and that they have clearly explained their reasoning in the **Math Text Boxes**.

   • Students who present their work to the class can be assessed on their ability to explain their method to the class, as well as their final answer.

   • Assess students on their participation in the class discussion.

Adaptations

   • Extend the activity by having students add a fourth page and compose pattern blocks to create a creature whose area is equivalent to 12 green triangles, and another creature whose area is equivalent to 14 green triangles.

   • Have students add an additional page, composing shapes to create two creatures with the same area, but a different number of sides.

Division Stories

★ **Grade Levels: 3-4 (Ages 8-10)**

★ **NCTM Principles and Standards for School Mathematics**

- Understands various meanings of division

- Understands situations that entail division, such as equal groupings of objects and sharing equally

- Selects appropriate methods and tools for computing with whole numbers

- Develops fluency in dividing whole numbers

- Models problem situations with objects

Note: These standards are listed with the permission of the National Council of Teachers of Mathematics (NCTM). NCTM does not endorse the content or validity of these alignments.

Description

Many students have difficulty with word problems because they do not know which operation(s) to apply to solve the problem. This lesson will focus on division. When students are regularly exposed to division in context, they learn to identify situations that entail division. Helping students *construct* division concepts in context, rather than learning how to divide and *then* applying context, will give them the knowledge and skills necessary to successfully navigate word problems with understanding.

In this **Kidspiration®** lesson, students will work in **Picture View** to explore the meaning of division through contextual situations. They will write their own story problems and use symbols to model the concepts of "total," "number of groups" and "number in each group." Students will be encouraged to explore both partitive models for division (when the number of groups is known but the number in each group is unknown) and measurement models for division (when the number in each group is known but the number of groups is unknown). Experience with both meanings of division will provide students with the flexibility to use and apply either to solve problems.

Instructions

1. The resources for this lesson can be found at the following location: **Kidspiration 3 Teacher menu>Teacher Resources Online>Lesson Plans>Grades 3-5 Math>Division Stories**. Save the Zip file and open the included *Division Stories-Produce.kia* activity. The class will write and model division problems in a whole class setting before students work individually.

2. Ask for a student volunteer to pick a fruit or vegetable from the **Symbol palette** that they would like to write a story about. If the tomato is picked, for example, ask students to think about how they might represent 12÷4 with a story about tomatoes and baskets. Which number represents the total number or starting number of tomatoes for our story? It may help students to see the total number of tomatoes; if so, demonstrate how to bring 12 tomatoes from the **Symbol palette** onto the workspace.

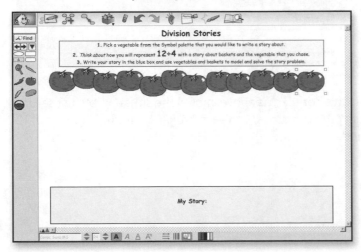

3. As a group, create a story about 12÷4 that involves 12 tomatoes and some baskets. Remind students that their story must contain a question; the question provides a reason for finding the answer to 12÷4.

Situations entailing division fall into one of two contexts:

Partitive ("dealing out" or "sharing"): See below. In this context the *number of groups* is known, but *how many in each group* is unknown.

Total: 12

Number in each group: unknown

Number of groups: 4

My Story:
Jane has 12 tomatoes. She would like to share the tomatoes equally among her 4 friends. She plans to put the tomatoes in baskets. How many tomatoes can she put in each basket?

For a story problem with a partitive context, as above, model the situation by first setting up the 4 baskets. Then "deal out" the tomatoes, 1 to each basket, counting aloud until 12 tomatoes have been partitioned.

Measurement ("scooping out" or "making bundles"): See below. In this context *how many in each group* is known, but the *number of groups* is unknown.

Total: 12

Number in each group: 4

Number of groups: unknown

My Story:
Jim has 12 tomatoes and he wants to give them away to his friends. He plans put together baskets with 4 tomatoes in each basket. How many baskets will he have to give away to his friends?

For a story problem with a measurement context, as above, model the situation by first bringing out a basket and filling it with 4 tomatoes. Then bring out a second basket and fill it with 4 tomatoes. Continue until all 12 tomatoes have been placed into baskets. It may help students to think of this context as "making bundles" of 4 at a time from the original 12 tomatoes.

Note: Each basket brought onto the workspace can be changed into a **SuperGrouper®** by selecting the basket(s), clicking the **SuperGrouper** button on the **Picture** toolbar and choosing "Create SuperGrouper."

4. After creating and modeling two stories, one with a measurement context and one with a partitive context, discuss similarities and differences. In both cases, the answer will be 3, but the 3 will mean something very different depending on the context. Their solution, which can be written by clicking anywhere on the workspace and typing, should not simply be the numeral 3; it should tie back to the context of the problem. Students will benefit from identifying each context as either "making bundles" or "dealing out" so that they can explore both options when writing their own stories.

5. Have students work individually or in pairs to write their own division stories. Assign one or a combination of the following activities: *Division Stories-School.kia*, *Division Stories-Gifts.kia* or *Division Stories-Cupcakes.kia*. As students are working, take note of which contexts students choose (partitive or measurement). Students are often exposed to more division contexts involving partition, so they may resort to the familiarity of the partitive context. If so, encourage them to think about another way to represent division.

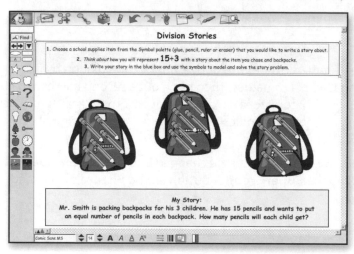

Assessment

- Assess completed activities. Exemplars representing sample completed activities can be found in the previously downloaded Zip file. Check that stories are appropriate contexts for division and that the concepts of "group" and "number in each group" are present in them. Models should correspond with the story and the written solution should answer the question in the story.

- Students can present their division stories to the class. Rather than showing their finished model, have students model their stories with symbols, acting out the "bundling" or "dealing." Classmates can also model each others' stories. Assess students on their presentation skills, their ability to communicate their reasoning and their understanding of situations that entail division.

Adaptations

- Adjust the activity to students' needs by changing the division problems to incorporate smaller or larger quantities.

- Students can also model division problems with remainders. "Leftover" symbols can be placed outside of the backpacks, baskets, etc., to show the remainder.

- Present students with a division expression and have them use any symbols from the **Symbol libraries** to write and model a story.

- For work with larger 2-digit, 3-digit and 4-digit dividends, model division in **Math View** using base ten blocks and **Math SuperGroupers™**.

- Instead of having students write story problems, the activities can be modified to contain a story problem, which students then model using the symbols.

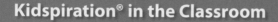

Parts and Wholes

✦ **Grade Levels: 3-4 (Ages 8-10)**

✦ **NCTM Principles and Standards for School Mathematics**

- Develops an understanding of fractions as parts of unit wholes and as divisions of whole numbers

- Understands situations that entail division, such as sharing equally

- Understands and represents commonly used fractions

- Uses models to judge the size of fractions

Note: These standards are listed with the permission of the National Council of Teachers of Mathematics (NCTM). NCTM does not endorse the content or validity of these alignments.

Description

Proficiency with fractions is critical to students' future success with mathematics. Before students encounter symbolic rules and develop procedural techniques for working with fractions, they must develop a conceptual understanding of fractions through a variety of contexts. This activity is intended as a first introduction to fractions and does not assume any knowledge of fractional notation or vocabulary. Students will have the opportunity to interact with fraction concepts in a problem-solving setting to develop their understanding of a new idea. Through the real-life context of sharing candy bars, students will use **Kidspiration Fraction Boxes™** to model and problem-solve. After their exploration, they will be introduced to writing fractions in standard form.

Instructions

1. Begin the lesson by asking students to describe a time when they shared candy or dessert with friends or siblings. Ask students to provide specifics—how much candy were they sharing? How many people were sharing? Did everyone get an equal amount? How did you divide up the candy? What does it mean if candy is shared "fairly?"

2. Open a new workspace in the Kidspiration Fraction Boxes Math Tool. Bring one fraction box onto the workspace from the **Math palette**. Explain to students that today they will help four students (Riley, Yolanda, Greg and Bridgette) figure out how to share candy bars equally. Tell students that the white space in the box represents the candy bar, and that right now it is whole, in one "part" or "piece." Ask students to describe how the four students might fairly share the one candy bar. To most students this will be obvious, and they will tell you to cut the candy bar into four equal pieces. Some might even use fractional language that they have picked up from everyday life, such as "cut it into quarters" or "cut it in half and then in half again."

   By completing this first, easier example together as a class, students will see how they can use Kidspiration Fraction Boxes to solve more complex problems. Show students how they can cut the candy bar into equal parts by using the up and down arrow buttons. With each click of the arrow, ask students how many equal parts the candy bar has been divided into.

   Be sure to go beyond four parts and back down again so students see that they can use the down arrow to reverse their cuts if they change their minds. Explain to students that the arrows allow them to experiment with different cuts before making their final decision.

3. Once the class has settled on dividing the candy bar into four parts, show how they can use the **Color** buttons on the **Bottom** toolbar to show the amount of candy that each student receives. Red can represent Riley's portion, yellow can represent Yolanda's portion, green can represent Greg's portion and blue can represent Bridgette's portion.

4. The resources for the student activity portion of this lesson can be found at the following location: **Kidspiration 3 Teacher menu>Teacher Resources Online>Lesson Plans>Grades 3-5 Math>Parts and Wholes**. Save the Zip file and open the included *Parts and Wholes.kia* activity.

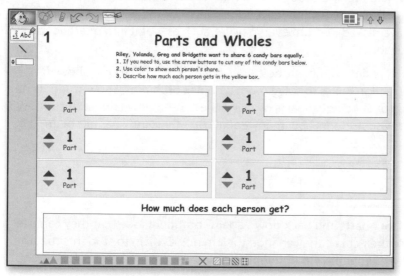

Explain to students that this time they will use fraction boxes to show how Riley, Yolanda, Greg and Bridgette can share six candy bars. When they are finished, they will write how much candy each person gets in the yellow text box. After students have solved the first problem, they can use the **Go to Next Page** button to solve more candy bar problems. There are six problems in all, and in each problem a different number of candy bars will be shared among the four students.

5. Decide whether students will work individually or in small groups. Each individual or group will need access to a computer.

    Note: If students are working in groups of four for this activity, they can complete the activity in the context of sharing the candy bars amongst themselves. When opening the activity, they can replace the names Riley, Yolanda, Greg and Bridgette with their own names.

6. Circulate as students are working. For the first problem, some students may decide to cut each candy bar into four pieces and then give each student one piece of each candy bar. While this is a correct way to divide the candy bars equally, encourage students to find a different way by making fewer cuts. Remind them that they don't necessarily need to cut every candy bar.

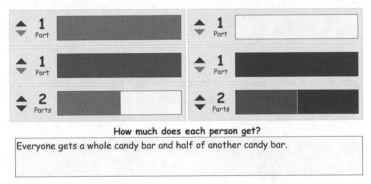

How much does each person get?

Everyone gets a whole candy bar and half of another candy bar.

    Watching how students record the amount of candy that each person gets will provide the opportunity to see what students know about writing fractions, whether with words, in symbolic form, or neither.

7. Once students have attempted most or all of the problems, have them share results for the six-candy bar problem. Did any groups do the problem differently? Some groups, for example, may have divided each candy bar in half and then given each person three-halves. Discuss why this amount is the same as getting one whole candy bar and half of another candy bar. Once students agree that the simplest way to divide the candy bars yields $1\frac{1}{2}$ candy bars each, write that quantity in symbols, either on the board or with Kidspiration using the **Fraction Frame** button on the **Bottom** toolbar. Explain why one-half is written as 1 over 2, without introducing the words numerator and denominator.

8. Discuss and show results for the remaining five problems. If time allows, have students present their answers. Take the time to talk about how groups may have approached the problem differently, making different cuts, while still dividing the candy bars equally. For each problem, ask students if they can now represent their answer symbolically with fractions as well as with words.

Assessment

- Check completed activities for equal divisions of candy bars. See *Parts and Wholes Exemplar.kid* from the previously downloaded Zip file for a sample completed activity. Notice how students initially described quantities in the yellow text box to track their progress with fractional notation.

Adaptations

- Extend the activity by adding additional pages to include four people sharing seven, eight, nine or ten candy bars. Alternatively, change the number of people sharing; for example, from four to three people.

Building and Estimating Fractions

★ **Grade Levels: 3-5 (Ages 8-11)**

★ **NCTM Principles and Standards for School Mathematics**

- Develops an understanding of fractions as parts of unit wholes

- Understands and represents commonly used fractions

- Recognizes and generates equivalent forms of commonly used fractions

- Uses models to judge the size of fractions

Note: *These standards are listed with the permission of the National Council of Teachers of Mathematics (NCTM). NCTM does not endorse the content or validity of these alignments.*

Description

Elementary students typically get a lot of practice shading fractions. On worksheets, they might be instructed to shade ¾ of a circle that has already been divided into four parts. For many students, this becomes a rote process of looking at the top number and coloring that many parts, without thinking about part-whole relationships or meaning. Students also struggle to conceptualize fractions because they lack experience making estimates about fractional size, and connecting symbolic and visual representations of fractions.

In this lesson, students will use **Kidspiration Fraction Boxes™** to dynamically build fractions by dividing a whole into parts and then using fill color. Before building the fraction, they will estimate whether the fraction is less than, equal to or more than one-half. Through estimating, students will have the opportunity to think about the relationship between fractions. The process of building will engage students in drawing meaning from the numerator and denominator. By the end of the lesson, students will understand standard fractional notation and its connection to a concrete model. They will also be able to describe and prove whether a fraction is less than, more than or equal to one-half.

Instructions

1. Introduce the activity by telling students that you have a brownie and that you plan to eat two-thirds of the brownie. Write ⅔ on the board. Ask students to estimate whether this amount is less than, equal to or more than one-half of the brownie. Have students describe, without drawing a picture or writing numbers, why they chose their answer.

2. The resources for this lesson can be found at the following location: **Kidspiration 3 Teacher menu>Teacher Resources Online>Lesson Plans>Grades 3-5 Math>Building and Estimating Fractions**. Save the Zip file and open the included *Building and Estimating.kia* activity.

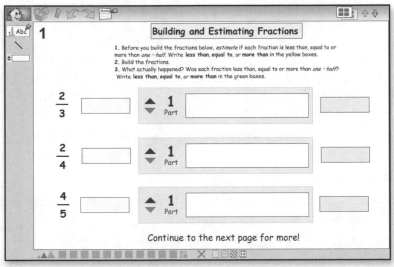

3. The brownie example can be used to complete the first problem together as a class. Read the directions aloud and then choose one student's estimate to write in the yellow text box. Explain to students that you will now build the fraction. Ask students what the 3 in the fraction ⅔ means. As necessary, introduce the term "denominator" as the bottom number in a fraction that describes the number of equal parts that make up the whole. Students might want to think about this as the number of equal pieces that are formed when the brownie is cut. Show students how they can use the up and down arrow buttons to divide the whole into any number of equal parts. Divide the whole into three parts, or thirds.

$\frac{2}{3}$ more than ▲▼ **3** Parts

4. Ask students what the 2 in the fraction ⅔ represents. Introduce the term "numerator" as the top number in a fraction that describes the number of equal parts of the brownie that you plan to eat. Show students how to use the **Color** buttons on the **Bottom** toolbar to show the two-thirds. Decide as a class if the fraction two-thirds is actually less than, equal to or more than one-half. Write the result in the green box. How can you tell that it's more than one-half? Remind students that you are not checking to see if estimates are always the same as the actual answer. You do expect, however, that students will think about their estimates and be able to give a reason why, as opposed to simply making a wild guess.

5. Have students work individually or in pairs, depending on computer availability, to complete all six pages of *Building and Estimating Fractions.kia*. As students are working, ask them to explain their estimates. The final page asks students to write and build their own fractions that are less than, equal to or more than one-half.

6. End the activity by going over each problem. Promote class discussion with the following prompts:

   • Were your estimates correct most of the time?

   • When estimating, how did you decide if something was less than, equal to or more than one-half? How did the numbers in the fraction help you?

   • Were any fractions equal to one-half? Which ones? Can you name a different fraction (not from this activity) that is equal to one-half?

Assessment

- Assess students on their reasoning when making estimates.

- Check completed activities for correspondence between symbolic and visual representations of fractions. See *Build Estimate Exemplar.kid* from the previously downloaded Zip file for a sample completed activity.

- Provide students with a list of fractions and have them estimate, without the use of a model, whether the fraction is less than, equal to or greater than one-half. Students can then check their work using Kidspiration Fraction Boxes.

Adaptations

- The denominator in fraction boxes can be increased to 36. Modify the template to include more difficult fractions, such as $18/29$.

- For additional practice relating fractional quantities, see *Almost Halves.kia* located here: **Kidspiration Starter>Activities>Math**.

- For additional practice building fractions and understanding numerators and denominators, see *Building Fractions.kia* located here: **Kidspiration Starter>Activities>Math**.

Comparing Fractions

★ **Grade Levels: 3-5 (Ages 8-11)**

★ **NCTM Principles and Standards for School Mathematics**

- Uses models, benchmarks and equivalent forms to judge the size of fractions
- Uses concrete and pictorial representations to develop an understanding of conventional symbolic notations
- Develops an understanding of fractions as parts of unit wholes
- Understands and represents commonly used fractions

Note: *These standards are listed with the permission of the National Council of Teachers of Mathematics (NCTM). NCTM does not endorse the content or validity of these alignments.*

Description

In this lesson, students will work with **Kidspiration Fraction Tiles™** to represent and compare commonly used fractions of halves, thirds, fourths, sixths and eighths. Students will have the opportunity to compare fractions that share the same numerator (for example $\frac{2}{3}$ and $\frac{2}{4}$), fractions that share the same denominator (for example $\frac{3}{6}$ and $\frac{5}{6}$) and fractions that are equivalent (for example $\frac{1}{2}$ and $\frac{4}{8}$). They will estimate relative sizes, build conceptual understanding through visual models, use relational symbols of <, > and = to make comparisons, and develop and discuss shortcuts for comparing fractions.

Instructions

1. Open the lesson by telling students that you are very hungry and that your friend has offered you some of their sandwich. The friend has given you two choices; you can have ¾ of their sandwich or ²⁄₄ of their sandwich. Write both fractions on the board. Ask students to think about which option you should take, and to justify their choice in words. Come to a consensus as a class and circle the fraction that represents the largest amount of sandwich.

2. The resources for this lesson can be found at the following location: **Kidspiration 3 Teacher menu>Teacher Resources Online>Lesson Plans>Grades 3-5 Math>Comparing Fractions**. Save the Zip file and open the included *Comparing Fractions.kia* activity.

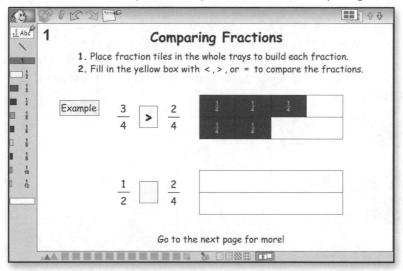

3. Read the directions aloud and talk about the first example problem, explaining that each amount of sandwich, ¾ and ²⁄₄, was first represented using fraction tiles. Discuss why the tiles are the same size, how many fourths make up one whole and why three tiles were used to represent the first fraction and two tiles were used to represent the second fraction. Explain how the yellow box was filled in with the greater than symbol, >, to show that ¾ is more than ²⁄₄, reviewing the meaning of the three relational symbols as necessary. If Kidspiration Fraction Tiles is new to students, demonstrate how tiles can be brought out from the **Math palette**. Also show students how to click inside the yellow **Math Text Box** and use the math symbol buttons on the **Bottom** toolbar.

Note: It is strongly recommended that for each comparison, students estimate which fraction is larger before modeling with fraction tiles. One suggestion is to have students decide which fraction they think is larger and mark it with color. To do this, click on the fraction and then choose a color by clicking the **Background Color** button on the **Bottom** toolbar. This process gives students the opportunity to reason about fractions based on the patterns they are noticing before they discover the answer with tiles.

4. Have students work individually or in pairs to complete all four pages of the *Comparing Fractions.kia* activity. Students will complete ten comparisons that involve halves, thirds, fourths, sixths and eighths. Each comparison will fall into one of three categories; either the fractions will share the same denominator, share the same numerator or be equivalent.

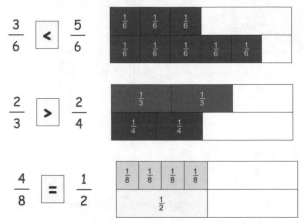

5. Conclude the lesson by having a class discussion about the patterns that students noticed while completing the activity. Include the following prompts in your discussion:

   • Did you compare fractions with the same denominator? What did you notice about the size of the parts when two fractions have the same denominator? (The parts are the same size, so the fractions are easy to compare.) When fractions have the same denominator, how can you tell which fraction is bigger? (The numerator tells how many of those equal-sized parts you have, so I know the fraction with the larger numerator is bigger.)

- Did you compare fractions with the same numerator? What did you notice? (Both fractions have the same number of parts, but the parts might be different sizes.) When fractions have the same numerator, how can you tell which fraction is bigger? (Since both fractions have the same number of parts, it depends on how big the parts are. I can look at the denominator, and the fraction with the smaller denominator has bigger parts.)

- What do you notice about fractions that are equivalent to $\frac{1}{2}$? What is the relationship between the numerator and denominator in these fractions? Based on this pattern, can you name another fraction, not included in the activity, that is equivalent to $\frac{1}{2}$?

Assessment

- Check activities for completion, correct representation of fractions and correct use of relational symbols. See *Comparing Exemplar.kid* from the previously downloaded Zip file for a sample completed activity. If students made estimates before completing each problem, check to see how often their estimates were correct.

- Assess students on their contributions to the class discussion.

- Students can present their answers to each problem. Assess presenters on their ability to communicate their reasoning about each comparison.

- Provide students with a worksheet containing multiple pairs of fractions in symbolic form, to compare using >, <, or =. Ask students to complete the problems by visualizing tiles and thinking about the patterns that were discussed.

Adaptations

- For additional practice comparing and ordering fractions, students can complete the activity *Ordering Fractions.kia* located here: **Kidspiration Starter>Activities>Math**.

- Modify the activity to include directions about first estimating which fraction will be larger (see the note in step 3 of this lesson plan).

Equivalent Fractions

⭐ **Grade Levels: 3-5 (Ages 8-11)**

⭐ **NCTM Principles and Standards for School Mathematics**

- Recognizes and generates equivalent forms of commonly used fractions
- Uses models, benchmarks and equivalent forms to judge the size of fractions
- Develops an understanding of fractions as parts of unit wholes
- Understands and represents commonly used fractions

Note: *These standards are listed with the permission of the National Council of Teachers of Mathematics (NCTM). NCTM does not endorse the content or validity of these alignments.*

Description

The concept of equivalent fractions forms the foundation of many other fraction concepts including comparing fractions, simplifying fractions, finding common denominators, operating on fractions and developing proportional reasoning. Proficiency with equivalent fractions requires that students work with a variety of models in a variety of contexts to develop both conceptual and procedural understanding. In this lesson, students will find and model equivalent fractions with **Kidspiration Fraction Tiles™**. They will use standard symbolic notation to write fractions, and reason about both numerical and visual representations of equivalent fractions.

Instructions

1. Open the lesson by asking students which they would prefer, an ice cream store that is ½ of a mile from their house or an ice cream store that is ⅘ of a mile from their house. Write both quantities on the board and after giving students time to think about it, have them justify their choice. Some students may pick one fraction over the other for reasons not related to quantity, such as "8 is my favorite number." Other students may decide quickly that the two distances are the same. Encourage these students to explain how they know this to the rest of the class. Introduce the term "equivalent" and relate it to other examples of equivalence they have studied. For example, what is an equivalent way of saying "half an hour?" (30 minutes.) What coin is equivalent in value to two dimes and a nickel? (A quarter.)

2. Go to **Kidspiration Starter>Activities>Math** and open the *Equivalent Fractions.kia* activity.

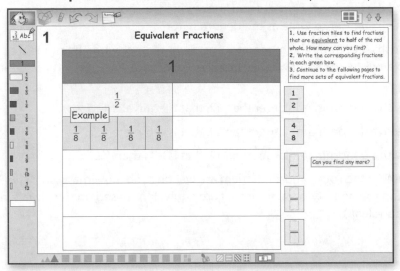

Read the directions aloud and talk about the example, explaining how fraction tiles can be used to find different fractions that are equivalent to half of the red whole. If the length of the whole tile represents a mile, the tiles help show how ½ of a mile is equivalent to ⅘ of a mile. When students do the activity, they will see if they can find additional fractions that are equivalent to half of the red whole, and then continue to the other pages to find more sets of equivalent fractions.

Note: If Kidspiration Fraction Tiles is new to students, demonstrate how tiles can be brought out from the **Math palette**. Also show students how to click inside the numerator and denominator of the **Fraction Frame** to write each fraction.

3. Have students work individually or in pairs to complete all four pages of the activity. As students are working, observe how they find equivalent fractions. Do they try each tile from the **Math palette** or are they selective about the tiles that they try? When students claim to have found all equivalent fractions, ask them how they know that.

4. Conclude the lesson by going over each problem and discussing the activity. Include the following prompts in your discussion:

   • Did you find the same number of equivalent fractions on each page?

   • How did you find equivalent fractions? Did you try each tile from the **Math palette** or did you only pick out certain tiles?

   • What patterns did you notice?

   • How did you record the fractions? How did you know which number to write as the numerator and which number to write as the denominator?

   • What is the relationship between the numerator and denominator when fractions are equivalent? (For example, 4 goes into 8 twice just like 5 goes into 10 twice. $\frac{4}{8}$ and $\frac{5}{10}$ are equivalent.)

   • Name a fraction, with a denominator larger than 12, that is equivalent to $\frac{1}{2}$.

   • Name a fraction, with a denominator larger than 12, that is more than $\frac{1}{2}$.

   • Name a fraction, with a denominator larger than 12, that is less than $\frac{1}{2}$.

   • If there are 20 people in the room and $\frac{3}{4}$ of them are wearing red, how many students are wearing red? Can you write two fractions that are equivalent based on this situation? ($\frac{3}{4}$ and $\frac{15}{20}$ are equivalent.)

Assessment

- Give students a list of four different fractions and ask them to find at least two equivalent fractions for each fraction listed.

- Check finished activities for completeness and correct fractional notation. For a sample completed activity, go to **Kidspiration 3 Teacher menu>Teacher Resources Online>Lesson Plans>Grades 3-5 Math>Equivalent Fractions** and open *Equiv_Fractions_Exemplar.kid*.

- Assess students on their contributions to class discussions.

Adaptations

- For a challenge after students have completed the activity, have them find *combinations* of tiles that are equivalent to the given fractions. For example, ⅙ + ²⁄₁₂ is equivalent to ⅓.

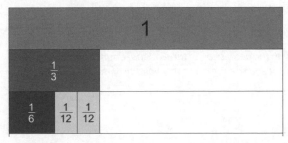

- Extend the activity by having students use pattern blocks to build fractions and find equivalencies. See *Pattern Block Fractions.kia* located here: **Kidspiration Starter>Activities>Math**.

Finding Factors with Rectangles

✦ **Grade Levels: 3-5 (Ages 8-11)**

✦ **NCTM Principles and Standards for School Mathematics**

- Understands attributes such as length, area, and perimeter, and selects appropriate units for measuring each attribute

- Develops, understands and uses formulas to find areas of rectangles

- Understands various meanings of multiplication and division

- Identifies and uses relationships between operations, such as division as the inverse of multiplication, to solve problems

- Develops fluency with basic number combinations for multiplication and division

- Develops vocabulary to describe two-dimensional shapes

- Builds and draws geometric objects

Note: These standards are listed with the permission of the National Council of Teachers of Mathematics (NCTM). NCTM does not endorse the content or validity of these alignments.

Description

In this lesson, students will connect ideas in geometry, measurement and number in a problem-solving setting. Through the real-life context of planning a garden, students will use **Kidspiration Color Tiles™** to build all possible rectangles with a fixed area on a grid. By recording multiplication facts that correspond with each rectangle, students will relate dimensions of rectangles to the concept of factors. Their investigation will help them develop ideas about scale, the commutative property, multiplication and area. This lesson can easily be extended to include perimeter.

Instructions

1. Open the lesson by asking students to imagine that they are planning a garden, perhaps in their own backyard or at a local community garden. Their garden must be a single rectangle, with an area of 12 square feet. Have students describe attributes of a rectangle and review the meaning of area as necessary, using the definition in context, such as "the amount of space that the garden can take up." Inform students that the side lengths of their rectangular plot must be in whole feet. A garden plot cannot, for example, have a side length of $6\frac{1}{2}$ feet. Ask students to estimate how many different garden plots are possible given these requirements.

2. Inform students that they will use a grid to plan their garden. Open a new workspace in the Kidspiration Color Tiles Math Tool. Select the **Show Background Grid** button on the **Bottom** toolbar to add a grid to the workspace. Ask if there is enough space on the grid to build a rectangle with an area of 12 square feet. Discuss how many people, including architects and cartographers, use small models to plan or represent something larger.

    In this model, each square will represent 1 square foot. Use a **Math Text Box** to write "1 square unit=1 square foot." Ask students why this information is important. Could a square stand for something else, such as a square inch, a square meter, or a square mile? Discuss how maps and blueprints always list the scale so that the reader knows the true distance or size.

3. Ask students to think about one way that they might build their rectangular garden using 12 square units. Elicit suggestions for representing this with color tiles, asking for specific information such as "use 1 long row of 12 tiles," or "build it with 2 columns of 6 tiles." Demonstrate how to drag tiles from the **Math palette** to build each rectangle. Continue until students are sure that they have represented all possible *different* rectangular gardens.

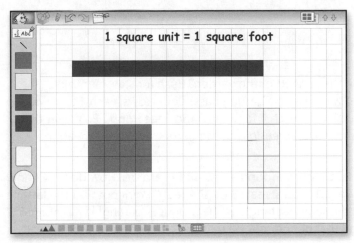

Notes:

- Rectangles with the same dimensions but different orientations, as shown below, are by definition the *same* rectangle.

- Rectangles can easily be moved to a different spot on the grid by multi-selecting all of the tiles you wish to move. Hold down the **Shift** key, click each tile and then drag the tiles until they snap into a new place on the grid. Alternatively, click somewhere outside of the rectangle and then drag your cursor around all of the tiles before moving them.

4. Ask students to think of a number sentence that describes each rectangle. For the rectangle that is 4 units by 3 units, for example, students might suggest "4+4+4=12" to represent the 3 rows of 4 or "4x3=12." You may choose to record any and all appropriate and representative number sentences next to each rectangle, but encourage students to think multiplicatively and come up with a multiplication sentence that describes the garden. Demonstrate how to use a **Math Text Box** and operators from the **Bottom** toolbar to record the number sentence(s) next to each rectangle.

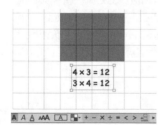

What does the 4x3 represent in the context of the garden? Push for statements like "the garden is 4 feet long and 3 feet wide" or "the garden has 3 equal rows, each 1 foot wide and 4 feet long" or "it has 4 equal rows, each 1 foot wide and 3 feet long." Point out that a multiplication sentence represents the *dimensions* of the garden. Does 4x3 mean the same thing as 3x4?

5. Ask students if they are sure that they have found all possible gardens. How do they know? Do we have a garden with a side of 1 foot? 2 feet? 3 feet? 4 feet? (Point out that the latter two side lengths are found on the same rectangle.) What about a rectangle with a side length of 5 feet? Are we missing that one? It may be helpful to build this to show visually

why 5 is *not* a factor of 12. Build a rectangle with a length of 5 tiles and count the tiles up to 12. What happens? Is this a rectangle? 5x2 is less than 12 and 5x3 is more than 12. Given the requirement that side lengths be in whole feet, 5 cannot be a side length of a rectangular garden with an area of 12 square units.

Continue listing potential side lengths up to 12 so that students recognize that they have rectangles with side lengths of 1, 2, 3, 4, 6 and 12 but not rectangles with side lengths of 5, 7, 8, 9, 10 and 11. As necessary, build non-rectangles so that students can eliminate side lengths that are not factors of 12 to confirm that all possible rectangles have been found. (Optional: If you wanted to surround your garden with a fence, which plot would require the least amount of fencing?)

6. Explain to students that they are now going to come up with possibilities for other gardens with different areas. Depending on computer availability, have students work individually or in pairs to complete the activity *Exploring Area.kia* located here: **Kidspiration Starter>Activities>Math**. The example on the first page shows rectangles with areas of 12 square units. On subsequent pages, students will build rectangles with areas of 10, 16 and 15 square units respectively. See the adaptations section of this lesson plan for optional modifications to the activity's instructions.

Note: On page 3, when students build rectangles with 16 square units, they may need help determining that a square is also a rectangle. Discuss the attribute that makes a square a special kind of rectangle.

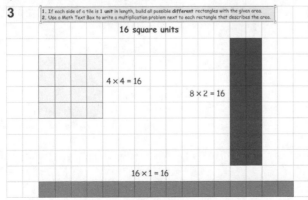

7. Conclude the activity by showing a completed project or having students present their work. Include the following in your discussion:

   • Were there any side lengths that were common to more than one area? (For example, 5 feet is a dimension common to gardens with areas of 10 square feet *and* gardens with areas of 15 square feet. Discuss the meaning of "common factor.")

   • Was there a side length that worked for *all* of the areas? (A side length of 1 is always possible. Every number can be broken down into 1 times itself.)

   • Were you able to make square gardens in every case? Why or why not?

   • Did everyone in the class have rectangles that looked alike? (Discuss how students may have oriented their rectangles differently while still building the *same* rectangle.)

Assessment

   • Ask students to find, without using color tiles, all possible whole-number dimensions for rectangles with other areas, such as 24 square units.

   • Assess students on their completed activities. Check that they have built all possible rectangles and that their number sentences correspond with their models. For a sample completed activity, go to **Kidspiration 3 Teacher menu>Teacher Resources Online>Lesson Plans>Grades 3-5 Math>Exploring Area** and open *Exploring_Area_Exemplar.kid*.

Adaptations

- Consider modifying the instructions on *Exploring Area.kia* to include any or all of the following:

  - List two multiplication number sentences that describe each rectangle.

  - Write all possible number sentences that describe each rectangle.

  - Find the perimeter as well as the area. How much fencing would it take to surround each plot?

  - Write about which garden plot you would choose and why.

- Add more pages to the activity and model other areas. Tile and grid size can be modified using the **Resize Manipulatives** button.

- For additional practice representing basic multiplication facts with arrays, see *Building Arrays.kia* located here: **Kidspiration Starter>Activities>Math**.

Flips, Slides and Turns

⭐ **Grade Levels: 3-5 (Ages 8-11)**

⭐ **NCTM Principles and Standards for School Mathematics**

- Recognizes, predicts, describes and applies flips, slides and turns of two-dimensional shapes
- Describes location and movement using common language and geometric vocabulary
- Investigates, describes and reasons about the results of transforming shapes
- Explores congruence and symmetry
- Builds and draws geometric objects

Note: These standards are listed with the permission of the National Council of Teachers of Mathematics (NCTM). NCTM does not endorse the content or validity of these alignments.

Description

Explorations with transformations are an important part of spatial learning and geometric reasoning in the primary grades. In this lesson, students will use **Kidspiration Color Tiles™** on a grid to investigate flips (reflections), slides (translations), and turns (rotations). By building figures and reasoning about motion, position, orientation, shape, and size, students will deepen their understanding of two-dimensional space. They will also develop their geometric vocabulary and make connections to symmetry and congruence.

Instructions

1. The resources for this lesson can be found at the following location: **Kidspiration 3 Teacher menu>Teacher Resources Online>Lesson Plans>Grades 3-5 Math>Flips, Slides and Turns**. Save the Zip file and open the included *Flips Slides and Turns.kia* activity.

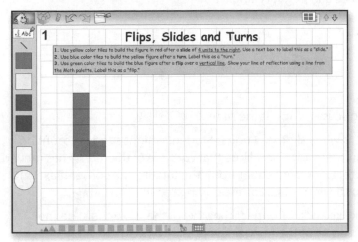

It may be beneficial to complete the first page as a class before having students work independently. Ask students what the red figure resembles (the letter L.) Explain to students that they are going to use color tiles to build the red figure after a series of transformations, also known as flips, slides and turns.

2. Read the first instruction aloud and elicit suggestions from students as to how they can use color tiles to build the "L" after a slide of 4 units to the right. What does a slide mean? Ask students to put their hands in the air with their fingers pointing up and show a slide of their hand. Discuss how some students may have used a hand motion to show a slide up, down, right, left, or even diagonally. All of these are slides; no matter how students slid their hands, their fingers were still pointing up after the slide.

Ask for a student volunteer to use yellow color tiles to build the red "L" after a slide of 4 units to the right. Have other students participate and make suggestions, making adjustments to the image as necessary. Demonstrate how to use a **Math Text Box** to write "slide" next to the yellow figure. Students can either bring out a text box from the **Math palette** or simply click anywhere on the workspace and begin typing.

3. Include the following in your discussion about the slide:

    • How can we be sure that this was a slide of 4 units? Students might suggest counting the grid squares. Where can we count from? Note that *each* tile of the red "L" has moved 4 units to the right; no matter where you count from (the top tile, the corner tile, etc.), each yellow tile is 4 units to the right of its corresponding red tile.

    • Does the yellow figure look like an "L"? Connect the slide of the "L" to the slide they showed with the hands earlier. All of their fingers were still pointing the same direction after a slide. Here, the long part of the yellow "L," after the slide, is still pointing up, just as the long part of the red "L" was pointing up.

4. Read the second instruction aloud and ask students to describe a turn. Have them put their hands in the air, fingers pointing up, and show a turn, as though their fingers are a clock's hand and their wrist is the center of the clock. Discuss how some may have turned their hands a little and others may have turned their hands a lot. In any case, unless they turned a full circle, their fingers are pointing a different direction from when they started. Ask for a student volunteer to use blue color tiles to build the yellow "L" after a turn. Use a **Math Text Box** to label the turn.

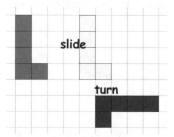

Note: The turns in this activity are open-ended and do not specify a center of rotation or the degree and direction of the turn. The activity instructions can be modified for more specificity.

5. Include the following in your discussion about the turn:

   • How did it turn? Did it turn a half circle, a full circle, a quarter circle? Compare this with the movement of hands on a clock.

   • How does the blue figure look compared to the yellow figure? Does it still look like an "L"? (For example, it is lying on its side and the long part of the "L" is pointing a different direction, but it is still the same shape.)

6. Read the third instruction aloud and ask students to describe a flip. Have them put their hands in the air again, fingers pointing up, and imagine a line running alongside their pinky finger. Ask them to show a flip of their hand over that line. What happened? How does the flipped hand compare to the hand in its original position?

   Ask for a student volunteer to drag a line from the **Math palette** onto the workspace and position it so that it becomes a vertical line over which the blue figure can be flipped. By holding down the **Shift** key while dragging the line, it can easily be moved to horizontal or vertical positions. Have the volunteer use green tiles to build the blue image after a "flip" over the line. Use a **Math Text Box** to label the flip.

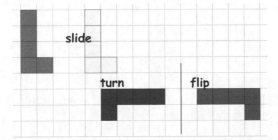

7. Include the following in your discussion about the flip:

   • What does the figure look like once it is flipped? How is this similar to looking in a mirror?

   • Could we have placed the vertical line in a different location? How would that affect the result?

8. Have students work individually or in pairs to complete *Flips Slides and Turns.kia*. The activity includes 6 pages, each containing a different letter and a series of transformations (flip, slide and turn) in varying order.

Note: If students need more room to represent their flips, slides or turns, they can reduce the size of their color tiles and access more grid space with the **Resize Manipulatives** button on the **Bottom** toolbar. The red tiles that are initially on the workspace must be unlocked from the **Teacher** menu before objects can be resized.

9. Conclude the lesson by sharing a completed activity or by having students present their work. For the transformations you choose to discuss, include questions similar to those posed about the "L," as well as the questions below:

   • Does a figure ever get bigger or smaller with a flip, slide or turn? (Flips, slides and turns alter the position and/or orientation of shapes but leave their form and size unchanged.) Discuss what it means for figures to be *congruent*.

   • Why does the final image, the green figure, end up in different places for different students? Are there choices students make about flips, slides and turns that affect the location of the final image?

   • For flips, did anyone place their line of reflection through the figure or touching it? How does that affect the image?

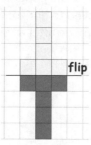

   • For turns, what were the different kinds of turns chosen by the students? Were there some that were less than a half turn, or more than a half turn?

   • For the slide on page 5, how did you make a "diagonal slide?" What does that mean? Did different students choose different directions?

- Look at the flip of the letter "H" on page 4. What other transformation, besides a flip, could create the yellow image? (A slide.) Why does a flip have the same result as a slide for the letter "H"?

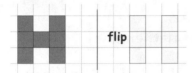

 Assessment

- Assess students on their completed activities. See *Flips Slides Turns Exemplar.kid* from the previously downloaded Zip file for a sample completed activity.

- Provide students with a series of images after flips, slides and turns. Have students identify the transformation for each image.

 Adaptations

- Modify the activity instructions to include specific information about turns, such as degrees and direction.

- For work with symmetry using pattern blocks, students can complete the *Symmetry.kia* activity located here: **Kidspiration Starter>Activities>Math**.

Adding Fractions with Unlike Denominators

★ **Grade Levels: 4-5 (Ages 9-11)**

★ **NCTM Principles and Standards for School Mathematics**

- Uses visual models, benchmarks and forms to add commonly used fractions

- Recognizes and generates equivalent forms of commonly used fractions

- Develops and uses strategies to estimate computations involving fractions in situations relevant to students' experience

- Uses models, benchmarks and equivalent forms to judge the size of fractions

- Develops an understanding of fractions as parts of a unit whole and as divisions of whole numbers

Note: These standards are listed with the permission of the National Council of Teachers of Mathematics (NCTM). NCTM does not endorse the content or validity of these alignments.

Description

Students often struggle with adding and subtracting fractions with unlike denominators because they memorize a series of steps without relying on number sense and without a connection to the underlying concept of equivalent fractions. In this lesson, students will use **Kidspiration Fraction Boxes™** to model addition of fractions with unlike denominators. By using the tool to build fractions and dynamically search for equivalent fractions and common denominators, students will develop the ability to reason flexibly with fractions. Their work with concrete models will help them retain and apply related procedures for operating on fractions with efficiency and understanding.

Instructions

1. Open the lesson by presenting a situation that involves the addition of fractions with unlike denominators and uses student names from the class. For example, Brianna bought ⅚ of a pound of fudge and Jeremy bought ½ of a pound of fudge. Record both fractions on the board. First, ask which student, Brianna or Jeremy, bought more fudge. How do they know? Inform students that Brianna and Jeremy would like to figure out how much fudge they have altogether. Does this situation call for addition, subtraction, multiplication or division? Why? Then ask students to *estimate* how much fudge the two students purchased altogether.

2. Open a new workspace in the Kidspiration Fraction Boxes Math Tool. Demonstrate how to use a **Math Text Box** and the **Plus Sign** and **Fraction Frame** buttons on the **Bottom** toolbar to write ⅚ + ½. Bring a fraction box onto the workspace from the **Math palette**, and ask students how they might represent Brianna's portion of fudge, ⅚ of a pound. What could the whole box represent? Discuss the meaning of the 5 and the 6, and show students how they can cut the whole (which represents 1 pound) into equal parts by using the up and down arrow buttons.

$$\frac{5}{6} + \frac{1}{2}$$

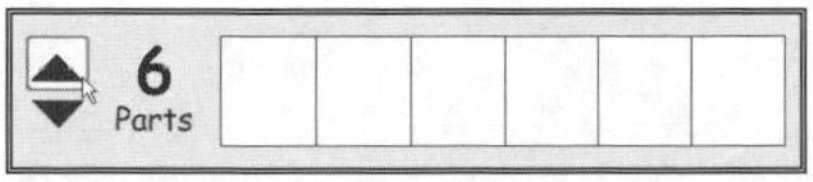

Ask students what each of these parts represents (⅙ of a pound), and how the parts could be colored to represent Brianna's share. Demonstrate how to use a **Color** button on the **Bottom** toolbar to represent the amount of fudge that Brianna bought. Bring out another fraction box and repeat the process with a different color to represent the amount of fudge that Jeremy bought.

$$\frac{5}{6} + \frac{1}{2}$$

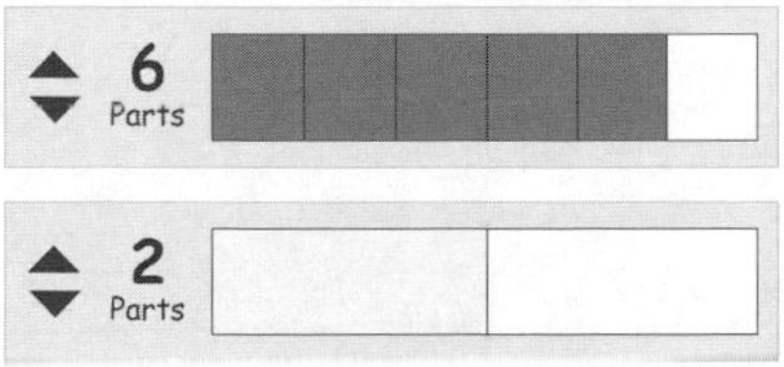

3. Ask students to refine their original estimates based on the model. Altogether, do you think they have less than a pound of fudge, about a pound, more than a pound, or more than two pounds? Why? Discuss any misconceptions about adding fractions, such as the common student error of adding these two fractions to get $\frac{6}{8}$.

4. Elicit suggestions from students as to how you might add Brianna and Jeremy's portions of fudge. How can we add fractional amounts that are not the same size? There are several routes to a solution, and depending on the suggestions from students and your goal for the lesson, you may want to facilitate solving the problem a couple of different ways. Two common approaches to the problem are outlined below:

Method 1

Some students might suggest that $\frac{3}{6}$ can "fit inside" of $\frac{1}{2}$, or that $\frac{3}{6}$ of Brianna's pound of fudge can be "combined with Jeremy's $\frac{1}{2}$ pound to make 1 whole pound." This concept of transferring a fractional quantity to "make a whole" can be demonstrated by multi-selecting $\frac{3}{6}$ and dragging them to the empty $\frac{1}{2}$ cell.

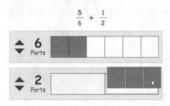

Note: A fraction box will only "accept" tiles if the fractional quantity being moved and the space to which it is moved are equivalent.

Does the model help us see how much fudge Brianna and Jeremy have altogether? Allow students to determine that the total amount is $1\frac{2}{6}$ pounds of fudge. If they are working on simplifying fractions, they can use the arrow buttons to "re-cut" the top fraction box and explore fractions that are equivalent to $\frac{2}{6}$. Once they see that $\frac{2}{6}$ is equivalent to $\frac{1}{3}$, click on the button that says "3 Parts" to officially change the top fraction from sixths into thirds. The simplified answer is $1\frac{1}{3}$ pounds of fudge.

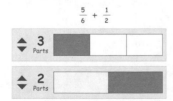

Method 2

A second way to show $\frac{5}{6} + \frac{1}{2}$ is to use fraction boxes to model finding a common denominator. Begin by representing each fraction, as before.

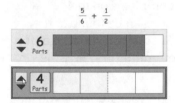

Can we find an equivalent fraction for $\frac{1}{2}$ that would make all of the pieces the same size? Show students how they can explore equivalent fractions with the up and down arrow buttons.

For example, $\frac{1}{2}$ of a pound is equivalent to $\frac{2}{4}$ of pound, but are Brianna's and Jeremy's pieces all the same size? Continue changing the divisions in the fraction box until students see that $\frac{1}{2}$ is also equivalent to $\frac{3}{6}$, and that both Brianna and Jeremy's portions can be thought of in terms of sixths.

To officially "re-cut" the bottom fraction into sixths, instead of halves, click on the button that says "6 Parts." Now that Brianna's and Jeremy's portions of fudge are both in sixths of a pound, the pieces can be easily combined. Drag tiles between fraction boxes to make 1 whole.

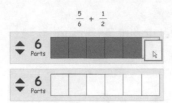

Ask students to determine, based on the model, how much fudge Brianna and Jeremy have altogether. If the expectation is that students also simplify their answers, for example, from 1²⁄₆ to 1⅓ pounds, they can use fraction boxes to model simplification as described in Method 1.

5. Use a **Math Text Box** to record the solution. Revisit original estimates and compare them to the solution.

6. Have students work individually or in pairs to complete eight problems on their own. The resources for the student activity portion of this lesson can be found at the following location: **Kidspiration 3 Teacher menu>Teacher Resources Online>Lesson Plans>Grades 3-5 Math>Adding Fractions with Unlike Denominators**. Save the Zip file and open the included *Adding Fractions.kia* activity.

Note: Depending on your curriculum, the goal of the lesson, and your students, you may want to allow students to solve the problems using any method. Alternatively, require that students find and model common or least common denominators before combining fractional quantities.

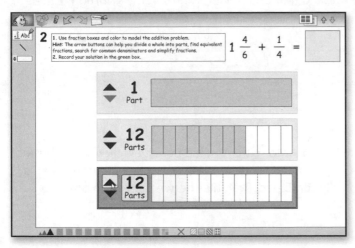

Assessment

- Assess students on their contributions to the class example problem.

- Have students present their solutions to the assigned problems. Assess them on their ability to explain their reasoning and justify their solution through the use of a model.

- Check completed activities for clear modeling of each problem and correct solutions. See *Adding Fractions Exemplar.kid* from the previously downloaded Zip file for a sample completed activity.

Adaptations

- Before modeling each problem in the activity, have students record an estimate.

- Add context to the addition problems by modifying the activity to include word problems.

- Add pages to the activity and create subtraction problems. Students can use the **Mark for Subtraction** button on the **Bottom** toolbar to mark tiles with an X and represent "taking away."

- The following activities can be used to differentiate instruction or extend the activity. All activities are located here: **Kidspiration Starter>Activities>Math**.

  - Students who need more practice adding and subtracting fractions with like denominators can complete the fraction boxes activity *Fractions-Add and Subtract.kia*.

  - Using fraction boxes in the **Step Workspace** can help students develop a process and a meaningful sequence of steps when adding fractions with unlike denominators. See *Unlike Denominators-Adding.kia*.

  - Fraction tiles can also help students visualize, understand and find common denominators. See the activity *Finding Common Denominators.kia*.

Area Models for Multiplication

★ **Grade Levels: 4-5 (Ages 9-11)**

★ **NCTM Principles and Standards for School Mathematics**

- Develops fluency in multiplying whole numbers

- Selects appropriate methods and tools for computing with whole numbers

- Understands various meanings of multiplication

- Identifies properties such as commutativity and distributivity and uses them to compute with whole numbers

- Develops, understands and uses formulas to find areas of rectangles

- Uses geometric models to solve problems in other areas of mathematics, such as number and measurement

- Develops fluency with basic number combinations for multiplication and division and uses these combinations to mentally compute related problems, such as 30x50

Note: These standards are listed with the permission of the National Council of Teachers of Mathematics (NCTM). NCTM does not endorse the content or validity of these alignments.

Description

In this lesson, students will use **Kidspiration Base Ten Blocks™** to solve multi-digit multiplication problems with rectangular arrays. By decomposing a problem such as 23x14 into (20+3) x (10+4) and further into (20x10)+ (20x4) + (3x10) + (3x4), students will deepen their understanding of area, the distributive property, and multiplication by powers of ten, while strengthening their ability to use, understand and apply standard algorithms for multiplication. Whether this lesson is used to develop an algorithm or reinforce conceptual understanding for students who have already learned an algorithm, students' concrete experiences with base ten blocks and rectangular arrays will help them make sense of the "why" behind the steps and tie computation to important place value, measurement and geometric concepts.

Instructions

1. The resources for this lesson can be found at the following location: **Kidspiration 3 Teacher menu>Teacher Resources Online>Lesson Plans>Grades 3-5 Math>Area Models for Multiplication**. Save the Zip file and open the included *Area Models.kia* activity.

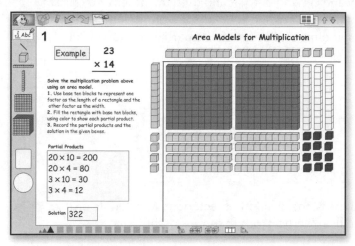

2. The first page of the activity is an example. It may be helpful to delete the base ten blocks and step through the example together. Begin by asking students to find an estimate for 23x14, giving them a chance to reason about the size of the numbers and discuss answers that would not be reasonable. Ask how they might represent each factor as a dimension of a rectangle using base ten blocks. Does it matter which factor is used to represent the length and which is used to represent the width? How can you show 23 using base ten blocks? 23 is the same as 20+3. How can you show 14? 14 is the same as 10+4.

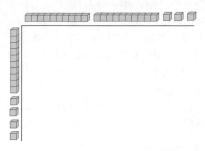

The inside of the rectangle can be thought of as composed of four smaller rectangles. Students will use base ten blocks to find the areas of the sub-rectangles, also known as partial products. For example, a rectangle with dimensions of 20x10 or 10x20 will yield an area of 200, as represented by 2 flats. Demonstrate how to select both flats, either by holding down the **Shift** key and clicking one flat and then the other, or by clicking somewhere outside of them and then dragging your cursor around both of them. Use a **Color** button from the **Bottom** toolbar to distinguish the partial product of 200.

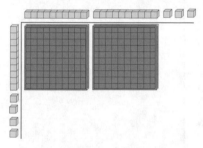

Ask students if they can find dimensions for another rectangle. A rectangle of 10x3, or 3x10, has an area of 30. Students can use 3 vertical rods to represent this area.

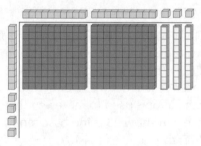

Continue this process to show rectangles with dimensions of 4x20 and 4x3. Elicit suggestions from students as to how they might use numbers and math symbols to represent what their model shows. Demonstrate how to use math symbols from the **Bottom** toolbar. Record the four partial products in the appropriate **Math Text Box**, and discuss how to find the solution from the partial products. Emphasize that the sum of the partial products is the same as the total area of the rectangle, which can be found by combining all of the blocks inside of the rectangle. Have students count the blocks to confirm the total area. Does this answer seem reasonable? How close is it to the estimate?

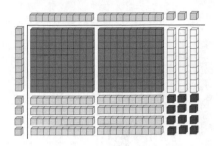

Partial Products

20 × 10 = 200
20 × 4 = 80
3 × 10 = 30
3 × 4 = 12

Solution 322

Note: You may choose to complete the same problem a second time to show that switching the length and width yields the same partial products and final result.

3. Have students work independently or in pairs to complete the activity. *Area Models.kia* includes ten multiplication problems, both single-digit by double-digit and double-digit by double-digit. Circulate while students are working, asking them to vocalize how they found each partial product and how their final solution relates to the rectangle they created.

4. Conclude the lesson by showing the area model for select problems or having students present their solutions. Compare different representations that led to the same result. For example, did it matter which factor was represented across the top and which factor was represented down the side? Did the order in which the partial products were listed matter?

5. Allow ample time for students to use rectangular arrays to determine area before connecting it to an algorithm for multiplication. On the other hand, if students are already familiar with an algorithm and are using this lesson to make sense of it, help students tie the algorithm to the visual model. Two of the most common algorithms are shown below:

"Traditional" Algorithm

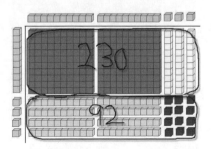

"Partial Products" Algorithm

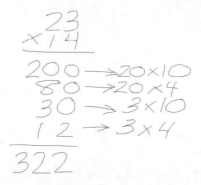

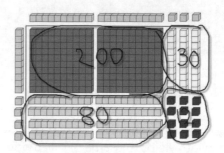

Note: Some educators and curricula recommend beginning with the partial products algorithm because the process more clearly aligns with the underlying place value concepts and the distributive property, both of which are at the heart of multi-digit multiplication. For example, instead of multiplying 4x2, the partial products algorithm involves multiplying 4x20, which accurately reflects the quantities being multiplied and ties more closely to the visual area model. However, the area model can be used to understand the traditional algorithm as well. Depending on your curriculum, your preferences and your students' level of conceptual development, you may choose to discuss one or both of the algorithms, or tie the visual model to other algorithms for multiplication.

Once students are comfortable using and understanding area models, tie the models to the development of efficient algorithms. Students who use the partial products method will also benefit from their work with base ten blocks when they transition to using an open rectangle to find the solution.

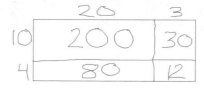

Assessment

- Assess completed activities for correct use of area models, correspondence between partial products and area models, and solutions. See *Area Models Exemplar.kid* from the previously downloaded Zip file for a sample completed activity.

- Once students have tied their visual models to a symbolic process, give them a multiplication problem to complete with pencil and paper. Have them solve the problem symbolically and then check their work with a model.

- Have students mentally solve a problem, such as 5x31 or 21x12, and then share their strategies with the class.

Adaptations

- Modify the activity to differentiate instruction. For some students, include only single-digit by double-digit multiplication problems.

- Students can record partial products directly on their models. This can be done by dragging a **Math Text Box** from the **Math palette** and placing it on top of the base ten blocks.

- Require students to record an estimate before modeling each problem.

- To give students practice modeling multiplication problems with larger factors, use smaller base ten blocks. Blocks can be resized with the **Resize Manipulatives** button on the **Bottom** toolbar.

- For more work with single-digit by single-digit multiplication problems using arrays, see *Building Arrays.kia* located here: **Kidspiration Starter>Activities>Math**.

Long Division

✦ **Grade Levels: 4-5 (Ages 9-11)**

✦ **NCTM Principles and Standards for School Mathematics**

- Develops fluency in dividing whole numbers

- Understands the place value structure of the base-ten number system

- Recognizes equivalent representations for the same number and generates them by composing and decomposing numbers

- Understands the meaning of division

- Selects appropriate methods and tools for computing with whole numbers

Note: *These standards are listed with the permission of the National Council of Teachers of Mathematics (NCTM). NCTM does not endorse the content or validity of these alignments.*

Description

Students often struggle with the standard procedure for long division because they do not learn it in tandem with a conceptual model that offers the "why" behind the steps. In this lesson, students will use **Kidspiration Base Ten Blocks™** to model long division. Using the **Step Workspace** to organize their process, students will have the opportunity to solve division problems using place value concepts. The problems in this lesson are problems that students should be able to solve mentally or with other methods; the purpose is to understand the process for long division using smaller numbers before moving on to larger numbers. The activity can be used as an introduction to long division, or with students who have already learned the procedure but will benefit from modeling the process to build conceptual understanding.

Notes:

- If this activity is used as a starting point for learning long division, omit the discussion about the standard procedure until after students have had enough time to work with concrete models using base ten blocks. Then, facilitate a discussion in which students, based on their work with models, develop an approach to solving long division problems in symbolic form. Tie their approaches to the standard procedure.

- There are multiple methods and approaches to dividing numbers, including successive subtraction, subtraction by powers of ten and subtraction by partial quotients. While this lesson uses base ten blocks to build conceptual understanding of the traditional algorithm, base ten blocks can be used to help students understand any division method.

Instructions

1. Begin the lesson by asking for three student volunteers. Explain to the class that you have 21 apples, and that you want to divide them equally between the three students. Ask students to come up with a division problem that represents this situation, and to describe how they would divide the apples. Have them act out the process of dividing, or partitioning, into three groups. Explain to students that while division is always about separating into equal-sized groups, it can sometimes involve very large numbers. This is called long division, and often involves several steps.

2. From the **Math Tool Starter**, check the **Use Steps** checkbox and choose the Base Ten Blocks Math Tool. In step 1, use a **Math Text Box** to write a division problem that does not require regrouping, such as **2)264**. Ask students what this means in the context of sharing apples. Students might respond that it means splitting 264 apples equally among two people, or making groups of two until all of the apples are gone. Students should be familiar with both interpretations of division. Explain that for this problem, they will model sharing apples equally among two people. Have them estimate how many apples each person will get.

Elicit students' suggestions in representing this situation with **Math SuperGroupers™** and base ten blocks, and then bring both onto the workspace to show 264 and two groupers. It may be helpful to color each type of block differently, so that when students work on more advanced long division problems they can clearly see the impact of regrouping.

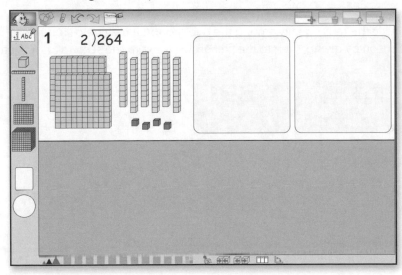

3. Now that the first step of setting up the problem has been completed, add a second step using the **Add Step** button.

   Note: In the **Step Workspace**, all manipulatives and **Math SuperGroupers** copy to the next step so that students can continue working on their model from where they left off in the previous step.

4. Ask students if they are able to divide the hundreds equally among the two groups.

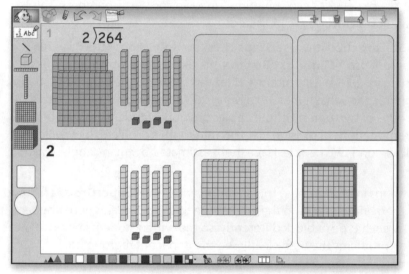

Add a third step and divide the tens equally among the two groups. It may help students to keep track of the distribution by giving 1 ten to the first group, 1 ten to the second group, etc.

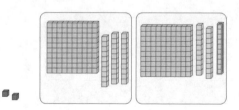

Finally, add a fourth step and divide the ones. Each group contains 132. How close was their estimate?

4

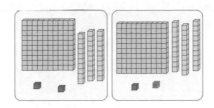

5. Use the **Go to Previous Step** button to navigate back to step 1, and then review each step in the completed problem using the **Go to Next Step** button. Ask students if it mattered in this problem whether or not the hundreds were divvied up first. Would you get the same answer by starting with the ones?

6. If students are familiar with the standard procedure for long division, ask a volunteer to come to the board and complete the same problem. If not, wait until students have worked with several models before developing the algorithm.

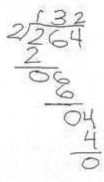

Discuss the relationship between each step in the long division procedure and its visual model. For example, in the problem **2)264**, what does the 2 inside the bracket really represent (200), and why do we put a 1 on top of it when completing long division? How does this relate to step 2 of the base ten blocks model? (Each person gets 100.) Why, in this particular problem, do we always get zeros when we do our subtraction? (Because each group of hundreds, tens and ones can be divided evenly into two groups, with nothing left over.)

7. Close the current document and begin a new long division problem in the **Step Workspace**. This time, choose a problem that requires regrouping, such as $2\overline{)132}$. In the first step, represent the groups and the initial amount as before, using color to distinguish each place value.

In step 2, begin with the hundred and ask students if the hundred can be divided evenly between two groups. Some students might suggest that each group gets 50; if so, ask them how the block could be shared. Show how the hundred can be regrouped, or exchanged, for 10 tens by using the **Break Apart** button on the **Bottom** toolbar. How many tens are there now? Can these 13 tens be distributed evenly between the two groups? Each group gets 6 tens and there is 1 ten left over.

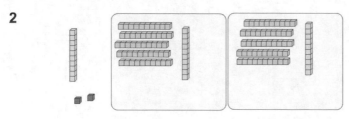

Continue to step 3, and ask students how the remaining ten can be divided. Break the rod into 10 ones and ask students how the 12 ones can be divided evenly between two groups. At the end, each group contains 66.

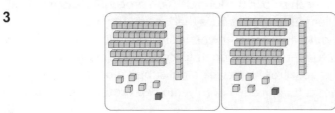

Note: You may choose to have additional intermediate steps that show the regrouping before the blocks are divided.

8. If students are ready, ask a volunteer to complete the same problem using the standard procedure, tying each step to the visual model.

Why did we start by dividing the 2 into a double digit, 13, instead of just a single digit as before? How does the step of subtracting, getting a 1 and then bringing down a 2 to form a 12 relate to what was just done with base ten blocks? Why does it matter where we place the 6's when we record the answer?

9. Have students work individually or in pairs to complete the activity *Long Division.kia* located here: **Kidspiration Starter>Activities>Math**. Ask students to look closely at the example problem before beginning. For each step, they will explain their work in a text box. For a sample completed activity, go to **Kidspiration 3 Teacher menu>Teacher Resources Online>Lesson Plans>Grades 3-5 Math>Long Division** and open *Long_Division_Exemplar.kid*.

 Assessment

- Students can be assessed on their participation in solving and discussing the two problems completed as a class.

- Check completed activities, paying attention to how students organized their steps and their written explanations for each step.

 Adaptations

- While the **Step Workspace** preserves each step in a step-by-step process, long division can be modeled using Kidspiration Base Ten Blocks outside of the **Step Workspace**.

- For more practice, students can complete additional long division problems using base ten blocks. Modify the activity, *Long Division.kia*, to include a different division problem, or have students start a new document and set up division problems from their textbooks.

Mixed Numbers and Improper Fractions

★ **Grade Levels: 4-5 (Ages 9-11)**

★ **NCTM Principles and Standards for School Mathematics**

- Recognizes and generates equivalent forms of commonly used fractions
- Uses models, benchmarks and equivalent forms to judge the size of fractions
- Uses concrete and pictorial representations to develop an understanding of conventional symbolic notations
- Develops an understanding of fractions as parts of unit wholes and as divisions of whole numbers

Note: These standards are listed with the permission of the National Council of Teachers of Mathematics (NCTM). NCTM does not endorse the content or validity of these alignments.

Description

Translating between mixed numbers and improper fractions is integral to success with advanced operations involving fractions, whether in arithmetic or algebra. In this lesson, students will use **Kidspiration Fraction Tiles™** to translate between improper fractions and mixed numbers. Students' work with concrete models will help them conceptualize what it means to translate between these two equivalent representations. After completing the activity, students will talk about the patterns they noticed and will begin to develop strategies for translating between improper fractions and mixed numbers in symbolic form.

Instructions

1. Open the lesson by asking students to imagine that their friend has just offered them $8/6$ of a chocolate bar. Write the fraction where students can see it. Ask students what is different about this fraction compared to most fractions they see. Then have students estimate how much chocolate they will be getting. Is it less than 1 whole chocolate bar? More than 1 whole chocolate bar? How much less or more?

2. Open a new workspace in the Kidspiration Fraction Tiles Math Tool. Use a **Math Text Box** and the **Fraction Frame** button on the **Bottom** toolbar to write the fraction $8/6$. Explain to students that they are going to model the fraction so that they can figure out how much chocolate their friend has offered. Have a student volunteer represent $8/6$ using fraction tiles.

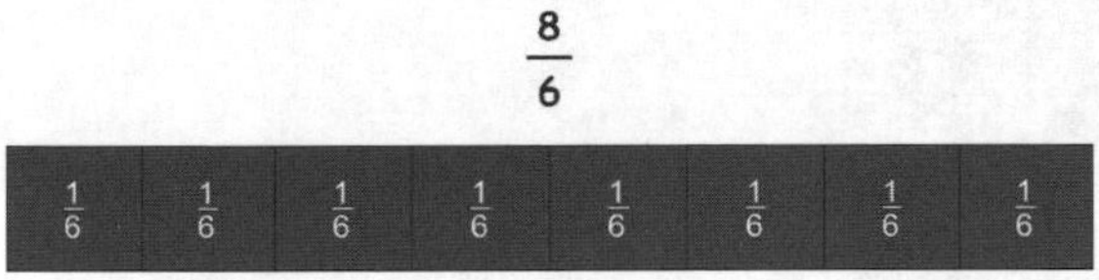

   Note: Drag each one-sixth tile onto the workspace and place them next to each other so that they snap into alignment. Alternatively, once the first tile is brought onto the workspace, simply click the one-sixth tile repeatedly (in the **Math palette**) and the tiles will align from left to right.

3. Ask students to refine their original estimate. Do they still think that this is less than 1 whole chocolate bar? More than 1 whole chocolate bar? Why? Some students may know that 6-sixths makes 1 whole, and will notice that there are 2 additional sixths. Ask for a student volunteer to justify their reasoning using fraction tiles.

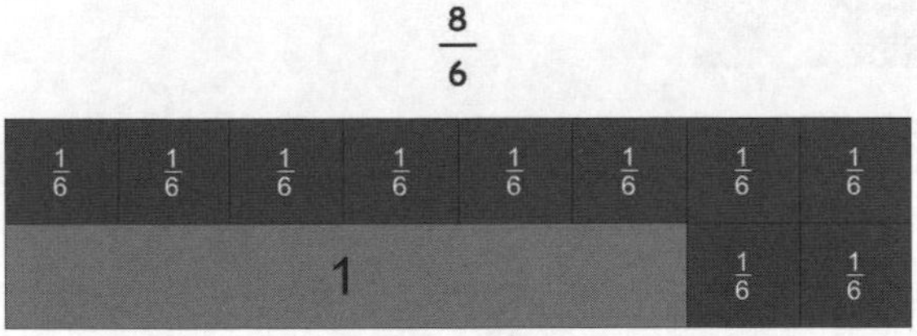

   - How many sixths are equal to 1 whole chocolate bar?
   - Is $8/6$ larger than 1 whole chocolate bar? How much larger?

- How could we write the fraction ⁸⁄₆ differently? ⁸⁄₆ is the same as 1 whole and ²⁄₆ more. How would we write that? (Click inside the **Math Text Box** and use symbols from the **Bottom** toolbar to write the fraction as a mixed number.)

$$\frac{8}{6} = 1\frac{2}{6}$$

- Does it change the answer if the whole chocolate bar sits on the right, or in the middle? (No matter how the chocolate pieces are arranged, ⁸⁄₆ is still the same as 1²⁄₆).

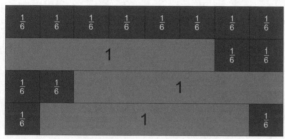

- Could we write this fraction in a different way? Is there another fraction that is equivalent to ²⁄₆? How can fraction tiles show this?

$$\frac{8}{6} = 1\frac{2}{6} = 1\frac{1}{3}$$

4. The resources for the student activity portion of this lesson can be found at the following location: **Kidspiration 3 Teacher menu>Teacher Resources Online>Lesson Plans>Grades 3-5 Math>Mixed Numbers and Improper Fractions**. Save the Zip file and open the included *Mixed Numbers.kia* activity. Have students work independently or in pairs. The activity contains ten problems in which students translate between improper fractions and mixed numbers, sometimes starting with a mixed number and sometimes starting with an improper fraction. All quantities are between 1 and 4.

$$2 \frac{1}{8} = \frac{17}{8}$$

5. Conclude the lesson by showing a completed activity or having students present their work. Include the following in your discussion:

   • Did you notice anything about the number of tiles that are equivalent to 1 whole? (8-eighths are equivalent to 1 whole, 5-fifths are equivalent to 1 whole, etc.)

   • Can you tell by looking at the improper fraction how many wholes will be in the mixed number? (For example, "From 17-eighths I can pull out two groups of 8-eighths, or 2 wholes. I don't have enough eighths to pull out three groups of 8-eighths because there is only 1-eighth left over.")

   • Can you tell by looking at a mixed number how to write it as an improper fraction? (For example, "If I start with 2⅛, I know that I have 2 wholes. Each whole is the same as 8-eighths so I have 8-eighths + 8-eighths=16-eighths. Then there is the extra 1-eighth, so that makes 17-eighths.")

 ## Assessment

- Check completed activities for correct models and symbolic notation. See *Mixed Numbers Exemplar.kid* from the previously downloaded Zip file for a sample completed activity.

- Give students several mixed numbers and improper fractions to translate mentally. Have them check their work with fraction tiles.

 ## Adaptations

- Extend the activity or differentiate instruction by having students explore addition or subtraction with improper fractions and mixed numbers.

$$1\ \frac{1}{8}\ +\ \frac{5}{4}\ =\ 2\ \frac{3}{8}$$

- For improper fractions, require that students use a **Math Text Box** to record the two whole numbers that they think the fraction falls between before they model the problem. This will force students to reason and make estimates about fractions in symbolic form before checking their work with a model.

- Depending on the focus of the activity, you may or may not require students to show mixed numbers in simplified form.

Representing and Comparing Decimals

✦ Grade Levels: 4-5 (Ages 9-11)

✦ NCTM Principles and Standards for School Mathematics

- Represents and compares decimals
- Understands the place value structure of the base-ten number system
- Recognizes equivalent representations for the same number and generates them by decomposing and composing numbers

Note: These standards are listed with the permission of the National Council of Teachers of Mathematics (NCTM). NCTM does not endorse the content or validity of these alignments.

Description

In elementary school, students extend their understanding of the base-ten number system to include decimals. Before students can add, subtract, multiply and divide decimals with understanding, they must represent decimals in contexts that promote conceptual understanding and emphasize place value. In this lesson, students will use **Kidspiration Base Ten Blocks™** to model and compare decimal values. The activity and discussion will allow students to reason through common misconceptions (such as 1.32 > 1.6 or 4.07 = 4.70) and compare decimals using models and standard relational symbols.

Instructions

1. Write two numbers, 1.32 and 1.6, where students can see them. Ask students to think about which number is larger, share their answer and justification in pairs, and then share with the whole class. Allow students to reason aloud without correcting them. Some students may assume that because 32 is larger than 6, 1.32 must be larger than 1.6. Other students might relate it to money; 1.32 looks like $1.32 and this is smaller than 1.6, which looks like $1.60. Explain to students that these numbers are called decimals, and that decimals are another way, like fractions, to represent numbers *between* whole numbers. Which two whole numbers is 1.3 between? What about 1.6? Tell students that they are going to model and compare decimals using base ten blocks.

2. Open a new workspace in the Kidspiration Base Ten Blocks Math Tool. Bring a flat onto the workspace from the **Math palette** and tell students that instead of letting a flat represent 100, the flat will represent 1 whole. Ask students if they can find a block that represents one-tenth. What does one-tenth mean? Guide students to make statements like "the rod represents one-tenth because 10 rods together make 1 whole. 1 rod is one-tenth of the flat." Illustrate the relationship between one-tenth and 1 by selecting the flat and using the **Break Apart** button on the **Bottom** toolbar to break it into 10 rods, and then using the **Group** button to combine the 10 rods back into 1 flat.

3. Ask students what one-hundredth means, challenging them to find a block that represents one-hundredth and explain why. How are the tenth and the hundredth related? How are the whole and the hundredth related? Reinforce relationships as necessary using the **Group** and **Break Apart** buttons. Once students are able to verbalize the relationship between all three blocks, delete all blocks on the workspace or add a new page to the document. Bring a flat, a rod and a unit onto the workspace, positioning them horizontally across the top. Explain to students that there is a way to represent each of these quantities using numbers.

Use **Math Text Boxes** to write each quantity in decimal notation near the blocks. Remind students that they already know how to represent 1 whole using a numeral, and then introduce the tenths and the hundredths places.

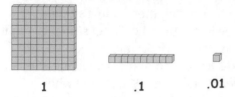

1   .1   .01

Note: If students are already familiar with the meaning of tenths and hundredths or do not need the review, skip steps 2 and 3 of the lesson.

4. Use a **Math Text Box** to write the two values discussed earlier, 1.32 and 1.6. Remind students of their earlier estimate as to which was larger. Students can refine their estimates if needed. Elicit suggestions from students as to how they can represent each of these quantities using base ten blocks. It may help them to think of each decimal as composed of several parts. For example, 1.32 can be broken into 1, .3 and .02. Say each decomposed quantity aloud as the blocks are brought onto the workspace; for example "1, three-tenths, two-hundredths." Select blocks and use a **Color** button on the **Bottom** toolbar to distinguish each value.

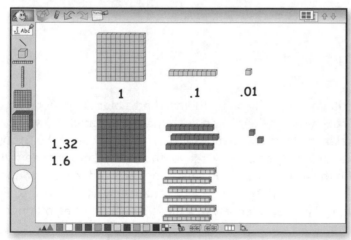

5. Ask students which value is bigger, 1.32 or 1.6. Why? How do you know? Does the answer surprise you? How is this different from comparing 32 and 6?

6. Have students work individually or in pairs to complete an activity in which they will represent and compare five pairs of decimals. All decimals involve ones, tenths and/or hundredths. Students will find *Comparing Decimals.kia* here: **Kidspiration Starter>Activities>Math**.

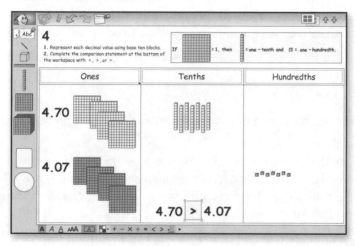

7. Conclude the lesson by sharing a completed activity or by having students present and explain their work. Facilitate a discussion in which students develop and verbalize "shortcuts" for comparing decimals. For example, "the value with the larger whole number is the largest number, no matter what comes after the decimal" or "if the whole numbers are the same, compare the tenths next because the number with the most tenths will be larger, no matter how many hundredths there are."

Assessment

- Check activities for completion, correct base ten models and correct use of relational symbols. For a sample completed activity, go to **Kidspiration 3 Teacher menu>Teacher Resources Online>Lesson Plans>Grades 3-5 Math>Representing and Comparing Decimals** and open *Comparing_Decimals_Exemplar.kid*.

- After students have had enough exposure to concrete modeling with base ten blocks, provide them with a list of several pairs of decimals to compare on paper.

Adaptations

- Require students to write each value in expanded form next to their representation. For example, "1 + .3 + .02."

- Add pages to the activity that include comparisons with tens in addition to ones, tenths and hundredths. Simply add a four-column place value mat to the workspace and label the column headings accordingly. If the flat represents 1, then the large block will represent 10.

- This activity can be easily modified to give students practice with thousandths. Use the large block to stand for one whole, the flat for one-tenth, the rod for one-hundredth and unit for one-thousandth. Use a four-column place value mat instead of a three-column place value mat.